William H. C Groome

The Fortunes of The Charlton Family

William H. C Groome

The Fortunes of The Charlton Family

ISBN/EAN: 9783337266950

Printed in Europe, USA, Canada, Australia, Japan

Cover: Foto ©ninafisch / pixelio.de

More available books at **www.hansebooks.com**

The Fortunes of the Charlton Family

AS THOUGH AFRAID IT MIGHT BITE HER.—*Page* 123.

The Fortunes of
The Charlton Family

Illustrated by
W. H. C. Groome

London
Wells Gardner, Darton & Co.
Paternoster Buildings

CONTENTS

CHAP.		PAGE
I.	PLANS AND DISAPPOINTMENT	1
II.	AN OFFER ACCEPTED	13
III.	BAD NEWS OF DICK	25
IV.	BROTHER AND SISTER	38
V.	DANDIE SEEKS HIS FORTUNE	51
VI.	IN A FAR COUNTRY	61
VII.	ADVENTURES IN POLAND	73
VIII.	FLIGHT AND RESCUE	83
IX.	A RIDE FOR LIFE	93
X.	STRANGE TIDINGS	107
XI.	A DISTINGUISHED GUEST	126
XII.	BRIGHTER DAYS	138

LIST OF ILLUSTRATIONS

	PAGE
AS THOUGH AFRAID IT MIGHT BITE HER *Frontispiece*	
'NEVER DESPAIR, DANDIE!'	47
AN INSULT WHICH DICK RESENTED	67
CONTRIVED TO DRAG HIM FREE FROM THE DYING HORSE	103

THE FORTUNES

OF

THE CHARLTON FAMILY

CHAPTER I

PLANS AND DISAPPOINTMENT

The quaint old ecclesiastical city of St. Andrews, Scotland, situated on a bold, rocky promontory overhanging the sea, never looked brighter than it did on a certain spring morning, many years ago, as a young girl of fourteen, with a goodly pile of school-books on her arm, walked briskly along South Street on her way to the Madras Academy. The sea, usually so wild and restless in that quarter of the world, on this particular morning lay gleaming like a mirror in the brilliant sunshine, now and then sending a tiny wavelet ashore, which broke gently against the frowning rocks on which the ruins of the old Castle still stand. A few golfers were already on the links, knocking their balls about, and arranging sides for a game. Three or four students in their scarlet gowns might have been seen leisurely wending their way to college, but no one seemed to be in a hurry. Indeed, it is the fashion to take life very easily at St. Andrews; so much so, that the very dogs on this lovely morning lay stretched at full length on the sunny street, basking in the unusual luxury of a really warm day.

Our little school-maiden, however, seemed to be an exception to the universal rule of taking things easily: a bright light sparkled in her dark eyes, her cheeks glowed with excitement, and as she caught sight of a young class-mate a few paces ahead of her she quickened her steps to a run, and overtaking her school companion she linked her arm in hers with a hurried salutation.

'Good-morning, Effie Moncrieff,' she cried; 'I have such news for you to-day! You could never guess what I have to tell you. This is my very last day at school! We are to leave the Priory next week and go to London.'

'To London!' exclaimed Effie, greatly astonished. 'What, all of you? Your mother, too? Why, I thought you were expecting your father home from India.'

'And so we do expect him,' said Laura Charlton, with some pride; 'and it is just because he is coming home that we are going to London. My father would never dream of living in a poky hole like St. Andrews. We only came here during his absence for our education. But he has written to tell mother all his plans. The letter only came this morning, so you may imagine what an excitement it was. He will arrive at Southampton in about a fortnight now. Meanwhile, we are to go to London immediately, take a furnished house, and be ready for him. Oh, it is delightful! I shall like London, I know. There is so much to see, and to do, and to enjoy. But—would you believe it, Effie?—Winifred does not care to go. She likes the Priory, and I do believe she would willingly stay in St. Andrews all her life, and yet she is a year older than I am. But Winnie was always queer. Why, she goes on Saturdays, our only holiday, and visits a lot of poor people! Faugh! I hate the sight of them! But Winnie never had any common sense—she is sure to be an old maid. Oh, Effie, don't you envy me going to London?'

'Yes, I think I do,' replied Effie Moncrieff, honestly. 'Still, I like St. Andrews. We have always lived here, you know; even grandmother was born here. But, Laura, you are only fourteen; your mother will certainly send you to school in London, so you won't have so very much time for enjoyment as you seem to think.'

'Of course I must have lessons,' replied Laura, promptly, 'but I need not go to a tiresome day-school as we do here. I shall have the best masters for everything—German, music, singing, dancing; but still I shall find time for sight-seeing, you may be sure of that. Oh, I do hope my father will keep a carriage! I'll tell you what, Effie, when we have settled down a bit, I shall ask my mother to invite you up to London to pay us a visit. Now, won't you like that?'

'You are very kind,' replied Effie, 'but I fear my mother would not let me go so far from home. But here we are at school.'

'Now, look here,' cried Laura, hastily, 'don't tell any of the other girls what I have told you till the luncheon hour. I want to tell them myself, especially that spiteful creature, Maria Jones; she will be so envious of my good fortune. I do like to be envied; don't you, Effie?'

But Effie Moncrieff was undoing the strap which held her books, and did not reply. The truth was that she did not at all care about being envied, she would much rather be loved. She was a gentle, timid little thing, a full year younger than Laura, whom she greatly admired, though Winifred Charlton would have been much more to her mind as a friend; but Winnie was fifteen, and Effie two years younger, and when girls are very young two years' difference in age is almost a barrier to friendship. She followed the triumphant and excited Laura into the class-room, and opening her books, gave as much attention as she possibly could to the French verbs. Her thoughts, however, would wander a little from the lesson to the grand prospects of her school friend, not in envy, but with regret that after next week she would most probably never see the Charltons any more.

Laura's head was also bent over her exercise-book, but when questioned by the master on the subject of the lesson her replies were so wide of the mark that she was twice publicly reproved by the angry Frenchman for her carelessness and inattention. Poor Laura! her little head was fast being turned by the brilliant prospects of the future.

Mr. Charlton, father of Winifred and Laura, was a land surveyor in Upper India, with a tolerably good appointment, and at this time was about forty-five years of age. He had married very early in life, but he had seen little of his own family, Mrs. Charlton having gone home with her twin boys and her baby girls fully eight years before our story opens. But the Charltons had never been a very comfortable couple. His was a character strangely compounded of good and evil, strength and weakness. He had been badly brought up by his parents, and on their death he had run through a fortune when scarcely more than a lad; still further to add to the chagrin of his friends, he had married a young girl quite beneath him in social position, whose chief attraction in his eyes had been her pretty face (although in truth she had one or two good qualities which he had not discernment enough to discover). Such a marriage was sure to end in disappointment, as this one did. The pretty face soon faded in the trying climate of the East, bad health and peevishness followed, till Mrs. Charlton declared that she must go home with her children, and then felt vexed that her husband was so very willing to let her go. In truth he was quite wearied of her complaints.

His marriage had been a disappointment to him; he had not found in it that comfort which he had expected, while the demands upon his purse had irritated and annoyed him. He had expected everything to be pleasant, with a good appointment in India, and a pretty young wife to accompany him thither; but here was disappointment indeed—an ailing wife, often peevish and unreasonable, and for whom he had not that devoted love which makes all sacrifices easy to be borne, and four children, all to be provided for out of an income which, to his extravagant ideas, was barely enough for himself. However, like other people, he was obliged to make the best of things; so when his wife insisted on going home, he allowed her to go, resolving to take up his quarters with a bachelor friend, and to fancy himself again a free man. Still, he had the heart of a father in his breast, and his eyes were just a little moist when he kissed his pretty little prattlers for the last time, and saw them all on board the steamer at Calcutta, on their way to Scotland.

Here we may say that both Mr. and Mrs. Charlton were natives of England, the reason that St. Andrews was selected as a place of residence for the family being that in the endowed schools of that ancient city a good and very cheap education was available to every one. It was also easier to live in Scotland on moderate means than in the larger and richer country, and Mr. Charlton, who had many debts unknown to his wife, was obliged to study a strict economy, if not for himself, at least as regarded the expenses of his family.

The poet has told us that 'Absence makes the heart grow fonder,' and in the case of Mr. and Mrs. Charlton there really seemed to be some truth in the saying. After a few years of separation from his family, Mr. Charlton began to long with a great longing to follow them home, and, feeling his own health to be in a somewhat precarious state, he wound up his affairs as far as it was possible to do so with this object in view; while Mrs. Charlton, recognizing a new tone of tenderness in his letters, felt her heart beat strangely as she remembered the many kind deeds and the good-natured disposition of the husband whom she had not seen for so many years. She resolved in her inmost heart to do all in her power to make him happy when they were once more reunited. But, alas for all the schemes of poor short-sighted human beings! How often we forget that the future is not in our hands at all, that the present only is ours, and that we are responsible to God for the use we make of it! The Charltons little thought that the anticipated meeting would never take place, that the husband and father would never again clasp wife or children to his heart. But so it was.

Two days after Mrs. Charlton had received that kindly letter which had caused such joy at the Priory, that letter which told of the speedy arrival at Southampton, a telegram was placed in the hands of the poor expectant wife, 'Mr. D. Charlton died suddenly, April 5. Buried at sea.'

How strange it seems when we think about it, that though death is the most certain of all events, the one fate which none of us by any effort can escape, it so often takes us quite by surprise! So much is this the case that it is the commonest thing in the world for men to neglect the making of any provision for wife or family in the busy days of youth or middle age, always imagining that there will be time enough for all such unpleasant duties when old age is actually upon them; yet how many never reach old age at all!

Mr. Charlton was quite a man of this kind. He was well aware that his monetary affairs were in much confusion, but he was only forty-five—

quite a young man as he thought—and he counted with unquestioning faith upon some twenty years or so of life yet to be enjoyed by him. During that long period he intended to do wonders: to make money, to portion his daughters, to set out his sons suitably in life. Alas! to think that the poor man was thus deceiving himself; when the hour was close at hand which was to see his lifeless body cast forth into the restless ocean, while the soul was called to appear before its God.

'Laura, you know that dear mother is coming downstairs for the first time this evening; do help me to make things cheerful for her; you look so melancholy, Laura, that I fear you will depress her sadly.'

The speaker was Winifred Charlton, a fair-haired, blue-eyed girl of fifteen, whose whole heart was occupied at this time with her poor afflicted mother, whose recent bereavement, with all the sad circumstances attending it, had brought on a severe illness of several weeks' duration, from which she was only now recovering.

'Come now, dear Laura,' pursued the elder sister, 'do cheer up a little, even the boys are taking notice of your depression. I heard Dick say to Dandie last night, that he could not think what had come over you, you had not a word to say to any one.'

'And why should I have a word to say to any one?' replied Laura; 'the disappointments we have met with seem to be nothing to you. You like St. Andrews, and are content to stay here, while I hate it, and will never rest till I can leave the place. Oh, I do feel so humiliated at school! that spiteful Maria Jones, I often see her whispering to the others and looking at me. I know very well what that means: she is pitying our poverty, and I can't bear to be pitied. Oh! Winnie, I am perfectly miserable! I can't endure poverty, and I can't bear to live on here for years to come, perhaps. Oh, I do sometimes wish that I were dead!' and Laura burst into petulant tears.

'Hush, hush, Laura,' whispered her sister, 'we will talk about this afterwards; but here comes mother, so do dry your eyes. Mother darling, welcome downstairs once more,' she said, affectionately kissing the poor, pale lady, whose once pretty face had sad traces of suffering. 'Dick and Dandie will be here in a few minutes,' pursued the elder daughter, 'and then we will have tea. The boys like St. Andrews so much, mother; they find it such a pleasant change from Dollar.'

'Ah, yes, my dear,' sighed Mrs. Charlton, 'Dollar Academy is rather a dull place, but, such as it is, I wish my poor boys could go back to it; but with our miserably reduced income such a step would be folly indeed. They must both work for a living, half educated as they are. Oh, it does seem hard! How it would have distressed your poor father!' And the widow shed a few tears, while Laura, who hated scenes unless she was the principal performer in them, crept out of the room, and betook herself to her own apartment, where, with a clouded face, she sat pondering over her own future prospects, which seemed to be poor indeed.

But we will leave the selfish girl to her own meditations, and turn our attention to the more amiable members of the family.

CHAPTER II

AN OFFER ACCEPTED

A few minutes after Mrs. Charlton had come downstairs, her twin sons, Richard and Alexander (or Dick and Dandie as they were familiarly called in the household), now lads of sixteen, entered the room, and greeted their mother affectionately.

'Glad to see you downstairs, mother dear,' said Dandie, ' and now we must take great care of you, and not allow you to be ill again. What chair will you have, mother?' he continued. 'Come and sit by me in the window, and Winnie will bring you some tea.' And he drew her gently to a comfortable couch, so placed that she could see the beautiful view from the window. 'And now, mother dear,' he added, with all a boy's impetuosity, 'Dick and I must soon fix upon our future course; school or no school, which is it to be, mother?'

'Which would you prefer, Dandie?' asked his

mother, anxiously. 'I know you love your books, my dear boy.'

Dandie hesitated a moment. 'Yes, I do,' he said slowly; 'but I know quite well that we cannot continue at Dollar now that your income is so limited. I am willing to work, mother; indeed, I have sent an advertisement to the newspaper asking for employment; but I scarcely knew what to call myself. A clerk? A half-educated boy, rather,' he added, a little bitterly. Dandie would have prized a good education.

His mother drew a letter from her work-bag. 'Alexander,' she said, in such serious tones that her son looked up almost alarmed, 'now that Dick has gone upstairs I want to speak to you very seriously, my dear boy. Don't go away, Winnie; you must be a sharer in our counsels. I can trust a great deal to your common sense, Winnie, and am thankful to God for giving me so kind a daughter.'

Winnie pressed her mother's hand, but said nothing. Young as she was, she felt very anxious about the future of her brothers, and she saw that her mother had something to tell, and she was not mistaken.

'This is a letter from your uncle,' said Mrs. Charlton. 'I received it only this morning; it is a long letter, as you see, and a kind one, too, considering everything. He offers to take entire charge of one of my two sons.'

'Our uncle!' repeated Dandie in astonishment. 'What uncle? I never heard you speak of him before. I did not know we had a relation in the world, mother.'

'No, my dear,' replied Mrs. Charlton, who seemed just a little agitated; 'I have never spoken of the past to any of my children. You were all too young, my dears; but I must tell you a little of your father's family and mine, that you may be helped to a decision as to your future in life. Dandie,' she added, looking rather nervously in her son's face, 'your father's marriage with me was in some respects a mistake for both of us.'

'A mistake, mother? How could that be?' cried both her children in one breath.

'Because,' she replied, 'he was a young man moving in good society, while I was a poor girl living in a very humble way with my widowed mother, a dressmaker in a little Devonshire village. Ah, my dears, it was a mistake. I could not make him happy when I was out in India with him, and sometimes I was not very happy myself. If God had spared him to return home to us I do believe things would have been different in future; but it was not to be. And I have told you this, my dears, because I must explain to you who your relatives are. You have two uncles; one is your father's younger brother. He lives in London; but though he has heard of your father's death, you see he takes no notice of us. He is not a very pleasant man I believe, and as there was a complete rupture between him and your father after our marriage, it is not very likely that he will ever do anything for you children. Your other uncle is my brother, Joseph Deane, and it is his letter which I received this morning. My dears, I don't know what you will say when I tell you that when I was married Joseph was only a shop-boy, a rough, clumsy, ignorant boy, though honest and good to our poor mother. From his letter I can imagine that he is much the same now as he was then, except for the difference in age. He has a shop of his own in Bristol, and he seems to be well to do. He makes a good offer, Dandie, for he says that if one of his nephews should agree to his proposal, he will take him into the business, and if satisfied with his conduct he will eventually make him his heir. He is a widower, and has one son, who has disappointed him sadly. The lad has run away from home, and his father has disinherited him, and wishes to put either Dick or you in his place. I knew you would not like this proposal, Dandie,' continued his mother, who noticed the cloud upon her son's brow; 'but I thought it best to let you know what your uncle's views were.'

'Yes, mother, of course,' replied Dandie, in a hesitating tone. 'What trade is my uncle engaged in, mother?'

'He is a spice merchant, Dandie; but I know my brother of old; if you entered his shop he would expect you to do just what other shop assistants do—wear an apron, and sell spice or coffee across the counter. Joseph never could bear the idea of any one being ashamed of his business.'

'I think he is right in that, mother,' said her son, heartily. 'No one should feel ashamed of an honest trade, but I confess I had no idea of all this, and cannot just in a moment make up my mind to take such a step as to agree to my uncle's arrangement. Will you give me till to-morrow to think it over, mother?'

'Of course, Dandie,' replied Mrs. Charlton, 'and do not give your consent too hastily, or only to please me, my dear, for, indeed, I can scarcely bear to think of you entering my brother's shop, it seems quite unsuitable for your father's son; but after all what can we do? We are very sadly situated, and very helpless, every one of us. Would Dick care to go to his uncle, do you suppose, Dandie?'

'Oh, no, I'm quite sure he would not!' replied her son, promptly. 'Dick has ideas of his own; he wants to go to sea.'

'To sea!' repeated Mrs. Charlton, sadly. 'What a life that would be! Of course, he could not hope to enter the Navy; it would be the Merchant Service, and ship-boys are so terribly ill-used. Oh, what difficulties lie in the way of my children! My poor, fatherless boys and girls!'

Here Mrs. Charlton, agitated by old memories and weak from recent illness, could not refrain from a few tears, which Winifred gently soothed away.

'Dear mother,' she said, 'you have talked too much and agitated yourself; put all this out of your mind for the present, and leave Dandie to think it over at his leisure. For my part I do not see why he should not go to Bristol for at least one year, if our uncle would agree to take him on trial; it would relieve you of a good deal of expense, mother, and do Dandie no harm; if he dislikes it very much something else might turn up for him before the year is out.'

'Really, Winifred, that is a very good idea of yours,' said Dandie, brightening up a little. 'I would not object to that at all, and I could carry on my education in the evening after the shop was shut; but I shall think it all over and write to my uncle to-morrow. Meanwhile I must tell Dick about all this; how astonished he will be!' and Dandie ran off to have a consultation with his brother.

Dick Charlton was by no means the same kind of lad as his twin brother—indeed, no brothers could well be more unlike than were these two. Unlike in appearance, temperament, and mental endowments; for whereas Dandie had a kind heart, common sense, and good abilities, Dick was never of the same mind for two days together, careless of the comfort of others if it interfered with his own, easily led to good if it involved no trouble to himself, but as easily led to wrong-doing if any enjoyment was to be got out of it. In short, Dick Charlton was his father all over again, and at this time of his life he would have required careful guidance if anything good was to be made of him for the future. He was bright-looking and handsome; much more so than Dandie, who was short of stature for his age and not particularly good-looking. Still, though mothers are said to be fonder of their handsome sons than of the others, Mrs. Charlton had always loved Dandie. Even as a little boy out in India, she had seen that the little fellow fully sympathized with her when she felt herself ill or neglected by her careless husband. And can anything be sweeter to a mother, or indeed to any one, than a tender-hearted, sympathizing child, who grieves over the troubles of the grown-up folk around him, which yet his young heart can scarcely understand? Such a child had been Alexander Charlton, and as he advanced in years still further good qualities developed themselves, for he grew prompt, energetic, and trustworthy. He was fond of his brother Dick, as was very natural, although quite aware of the faults of his character.

'Hallo,' he cried on that evening when he had heard his mother's explanations of the past and his uncle's plans for the future, 'here is a fine start for us all, Dick; here is a new-found uncle offering to take either you or me to his heart, and leave us all his money: why, it sounds quite like a play, except that on the stage the uncle is generally a villain who robs the unprotected little nephews instead of enriching them!'

'What do you mean?' said Dick, lazily, as he threw aside the piece of wood which he was trying to convert into a ship. 'We have no uncles, rich or poor, that ever I heard of.'

'Don't be so sure of that, my boy,' cried Dandie, laughing. 'I assure you my story is perfectly true, only our newly-found uncle annexes some conditions to the heirship which neither you nor I would care for. What do you say, Dick, to wearing an apron, and selling spice across the counter?' And Dandie explained the whole matter to his brother.

But to his great astonishment Dick did not seem to be at all unwilling to take to trade, or, in other words, to enter his uncle's shop in Bristol. He seemed in one moment to forget all his old fancy for a sea life, and to be ready to sell sugar or tea, or even to sweep out the shop, if that duty was also annexed to the situation. Now, how was this? Was Dick, thoughtful of his mother's slender purse, earnestly desiring to relieve her of the burden of his maintenance and to provide for himself, even in a way which to a youth brought up as he had been might seem almost degrading?

Scarcely so; but Dick had inherited from his father a great aptitude for spending money (though to earn it was quite another thing), and in this proposal of his Uncle Joseph he seemed to see nothing of the duties expected of him, or of his brother, whichever of them should accept of the offer; every such consideration was swallowed up in the enticing thought of the heirship. He immediately jumped to the conclusion that his uncle would be good enough to die in a short time, say, in a few months or so, and he saw himself the fortunate possessor of an inexhaustible supply of money. Of course he would at once give up the shop, sell the goodwill of the business, buy a horse and a yacht, and one or two other pleasant little possessions, and how he would enjoy himself! Oh, what a glorious life seemed to open up before him! But in all this there was no thought of his impoverished mother, or his young sisters, left to struggle with unexpected poverty as best they could; no thought even of his twin brother Dandie, his life-long companion and friend. His only thought was of himself. Alas! Dick Charlton was not the kind of son to bring joy to a widowed mother's heart!

'And so you really think you would like the kind of life?' cried Dandie, in amazement at the rapidity with which Dick had given up his wish for a seafaring life. 'Because you know, Dick, it would be an awful relief to me if you were really willing to go. I can't bear the idea for myself, but I had made up my mind to go for mother's sake and the girls'. It never entered my head that you would be willing to go, but if you really are I shall be truly thankful I do assure you. You had better write to our uncle to-day, and make everything plain to him. I think it is awfully good of you, Dick, for it must be a good deal of a sacrifice. I know I would have felt it so.'

Dick looked down modestly, and quite accepted his brother's tribute of praise as his due. 'Well, you know,' he said, 'one of us must do something, make a move of some kind, unless we are all to starve. Yes, I will write to my uncle this very day. He must be a jolly old boy I should think. I wonder how much money he has? But I say, Dandie, it is rather awkward about this prodigal son of his. Suppose the young beggar should come home again, and his fond father should receive him with open arms? Where would I be then? Head shopman, I suppose, under the lawful heir! Not if I know it.'

'Mother seems to think that her brother is a very just man,' observed Dandie. 'A little stern, perhaps, but strictly just and reasonable. He would never turn you out without some kind of compensation. Even if his son did return and inherit his father's money, he would provide for you in some way I feel sure. But, Dick, in case you should not like the duties after undertaking them, let me advise you to arrange with our uncle for a six months' trial. It is quite reasonable, and he is sure to agree.'

To this Dick having given his consent, the two brothers sat down together to concoct a letter to the Bristol spice merchant.

CHAPTER III

BAD NEWS OF DICK

THREE months had passed away since the conversation took place between Dick and Dandie which resulted in the former making up his mind to try his fortune as a shop assistant, or, to put it more truthfully, making up his mind to be his uncle's heir. The letter to Mr. Joseph Deane had been written, sent off, and duly acknowledged, the merchant formally accepting his nephew's services in the shop on the following terms :—

The contract was to be binding for six months, at the end of which time, if Mr. Deane were satisfied with his nephew's conduct, a more lasting agreement would be arranged. Dick was to live in his uncle's house, never to be absent from meals without permission asked and obtained, never to be out of the house after nine o'clock p.m. on any pretext whatever, to do in the shop exactly and promptly whatever his uncle desired of him, his remuneration being comfortable board and lodging with twenty shillings weekly, half of which sum was to be retained in Mr. Deane's own hand, and paid monthly to Mrs. Charlton as her son's contribution to the family expenditure at the Priory. The other ten shillings Dick was to handle himself, no account of its disbursement being exacted from him; his uncle, however, stipulating that it must cover every outlay—clothing, boots, etc., down to note-paper and postage-stamps. Dick was never to incur debt, even to the small extent of sixpence. If he wanted new clothing at any time, he must patiently accumulate week by week the necessary money before the purchase was made. He was to attend church regularly, enjoy a half-holiday every Wednesday, and if medical attendance was ever necessary Mr. Deane would pay for it himself. 'You may think these restrictions on your liberty hard,' wrote Uncle Joseph, in his letter to Dick, 'but they do not seem so to me, and I am a better judge than you can be of what is good for a young man not yet seventeen years of age. Besides, I have a special reason for not permitting you to handle all your weekly wages until you have a little more experience of the value of money than you can possibly have now. This reason I need not specify, but if I am satisfied with your conduct at the end of six months, I shall not interfere any further with your expenditure, but leave you to do what you please with your own means.'

Here we may say that Mr. Deane's special reason for not entrusting Dick with the outlay of all his weekly wages, was that he (Uncle Joseph) remembered very well the foolish extravagance of Dick's father, whom he had thoroughly despised as a vain, selfish man, and he thought it not unlikely that the boy might take after his father in these respects, which we have seen was precisely the state of the case. This, of course, he had too much good feeling to tell to Dick in so many words, it being always painful to right-minded persons to tell a son or daughter of the faults of their parents.

The arrival of this letter caused intense excitement at the Priory.

'So like my poor brother,' murmured Mrs. Charlton; 'severe, yet really considering your best interests, Dick, I do believe.'

'My best interests!' cried her son hotly. 'Mean, stingy, selfish old cur, rolling in wealth himself, and only allowing me ten shillings a week for everything I require! Why, mother, how can I dress like my father's son on twenty-six pounds a year, besides paying for everything else that I need?'

Mrs. Charlton took to tears.

'Dick,' she sobbed, 'you must forget your poor father's position in life, at least for the present. My brother had only twelve shillings a week when he was your age, and half of that he paid regularly to our poor mother, and he never incurred debts. My boy, you need not go to Bristol at all unless you like, but if you do go, I beseech you do not quarrel with your uncle. If you please my brother, you may be a rich man yet, and may give up the shop whenever you please!'

During this conversation between Dick and his mother, Dandie said nothing, though he thought a great deal. He felt that Dick, with his pleasure-loving nature, would never get on at Bristol. The two boys had been talking over things, as was very natural, and Dick had expatiated on all the fun he was to have after the shop was shut at night, the theatre at least twice a week being one of the items. Uncle Joseph evidently would not permit that, and to be kept within doors every night after nine o'clock seemed hard lines even to Dandie, for his uncle had no family, and how could poor Dick amuse himself? He did not care for reading;

even novels had no attraction for him—poor old Dick.

Dandie shook his head privately as he thought of all this, and almost made up his mind to try Uncle Joseph himself, and leave his brother free for some other chance in life; but on giving Dick a hint as to this, he found, to his great relief, that the prospect of the heirship still influenced his brother sufficiently to induce him to give Mr. Deane a trial.

'But it will never do,' whispered Dandie to Winifred, as brother and sister took a turn together in the garden; 'it will never do. Dick has no patience, and very little common sense, poor old chap, and my uncle seems to be as hard as nails.'

Winifred sighed. Young as she was, life was beginning to seem a vexatious problem to the gentle sister, who dearly loved both her brothers.

'We must just hope for the best,' she said. 'But I do think Uncle Joseph might have come here to see poor mother. Why, she is his only sister! I fear he must indeed be a very hard man. Poor dear Dick! I do hope he will be able to stand it all without breaking out.'

Now, breaking out, as we must explain to our young readers, was a very favourite practice with Dick Charlton, who was one of those peculiar young gentlemen who think that all the world ought to give way to them, not only school-mates, but even those placed in authority over them. On account of this disposition, he had often got into tremendous difficulties at school, and had fought many fierce battles with the other boys, in which, however, he had been quite able to hold his own, for Dick was a strong young fellow and by no means cowardly. But it had been quite a different affair when the overbearing boy had come into collision with the masters at the academy. Then swift punishment had descended on the culprit, and Dick had found it, on the whole, advisable to submit to discipline; at least, so long as he was a school-boy. At home, of course, he got it all his own way, as most lads do who are naturally overbearing, not very kind-hearted, and who have no one to interfere with them save a widowed mother and an admiring young sister, who, though in her secret heart she preferred Dandie, yet thought Dick's overbearing disposition to be a sign that he would certainly make his mark in the world. Well, we shall see if this idea of Winifred's was a correct one.

As we said before, three months had passed away since all this had taken place. Dick had gone to Bristol after a tender farewell from mother, sisters, and brother, and had written several letters home. But from the very first these letters had betrayed an uneasy spirit; he had chafed at the gloom of his uncle's house, the short dry manner of the old man, the wearisome nature of his duties, and the sour temper of the old housekeeper, his uncle's only domestic servant. In short it was quite evident that Dick was so miserable that his mother feared, and with good reason, that he would never be able to hold out till the six months had expired. Then a change had come over the position of things. Dick's letters, gloomy as they were, ceased all at once. Three weeks passed away without any communication with his home, though his last letter had been written to beg his mother to lend him some money, which we need scarcely say he received at once, though the family at the Priory had to pinch terribly in consequence.

'What can be wrong now, Dandie, with our poor Dick?' said the anxious mother one day. 'Three long weeks and no letter! Why, he has not even acknowledged the money I sent him! Can the poor boy be ill, do you think? Do advise me, Dandie. I have no one to speak to but you and Winifred, and she, poor girl, can do nothing but cry, she feels so sorry for Dick.'

'Perhaps you should write to my uncle, mother,' replied Dandie. 'You have written to Dick over and over again, and so have I, yet there is no answer to either of us. I think you should write to my uncle, and let us know the worst at once.'

Mrs. Charlton then sat down to compose a letter which might draw forth all the information required from Uncle Joseph, without in the least degree compromising her son. But, alas! while the pen was still in the poor lady's hand, she received a letter from her brother, which caused her to utter a cry of dismay and to sink back, almost fainting, on the sofa. But we may as well give Uncle Joseph's letter in full :—

'Dear Sister,—

'This letter, I hope, will find you in good health, as it leaves me at present—thank God for all His mercies! Your son Richard, since he came to me three months ago, has caused much disturbance both in the shop and in my household, so that long ere this I had made up my mind that he was quite unsuited for the position which I had intended for him after my death. I would, however, have kept him in my service till the stipulated six months had expired, and would then have placed him in some situation more suited to his disposition, but he has chosen to throw off all control, and, I grieve to say, has left my house without stating what he intends to do. One evening I discovered that he had left my house after nine o'clock (a distinct breach of contract), and had been seen in the theatre, my informant being a person upon whose word I can depend. He returned home at one o'clock in the morning, and entered my house as he had left it— by his bedroom window. When I spoke to him about this most unworthy conduct, his language was insolent in the extreme : he refused to make any promise of amendment, and finally returned to his bedroom and locked the door. Believing that it would be best to leave him to himself for a little, I went to my shop and attended to my usual business till a late hour at night. On entering my house again I was informed by my housekeeper that Richard was still in his bedroom, that he had asked her for some food, and she had taken him some coffee with cold meat and bread at seven o'clock in the evening. Being thus satisfied that his wants had been attended to, I did not disturb him that night, but resolved to have a thorough explanation with him the following morning, when his insolent temper would probably have cooled down. Next

D

morning, I grieve to say, Richard was gone. The bed had not been occupied, and some of his clothing had been taken away in a small carpet-bag. No letter or communication of any kind was left behind. I thought it best, before writing to you, to make every possible inquiry as to his movements, so as not to distress you needlessly. I have done so, and I have learned that he has sailed in a vessel trading between this port and Melbourne.

'He is, therefore, engaged in honest and respectable employment, though he will probably find that he has entered upon a much harder life than he has any idea of. If you will take my advice, sister, you will leave Richard alone for the present; he will come to no harm, and the hardships he is certain to meet with will probably have a good effect upon his unstable character. I tried to do my duty by your son while he was with me, but the result has been disappointing. I regret this very much, and if I can serve you in any other way I will gladly do so. Meanwhile, please accept the enclosed cheque as a contribution to your family expenditure.

'From your affectionate brother,

'JOSEPH DEANE.

'*Bristol, July* 14*th.*'

The distress caused to the Charlton family by this letter from Uncle Joseph was indeed very great. To think that Dick had actually gone to the other side of the globe without a word of farewell to the friends at home, the mother and sister who loved him so much! It was heartrending! And to think of him going on board a trading vessel as a ship-boy, herding with common sailors. What hardships he would have to endure, and what a long, weary time must elapse before they could hope to hear from him!

Mrs. Charlton was almost prostrated by this terrible blow, while Winnie, though feeling it deeply herself, was compelled to assume a cheerfulness which she did not feel, to prevent the whole family from sinking into gloomy despondency. But Uncle Joseph had spoken the truth when he said that poor Dick must be left to himself for a time; nothing could be done till they heard of the arrival of the *Shooting Star* at Melbourne. Whatever we may think of Uncle Joseph, and however much we may feel for a lively lad like Dick Charlton, compelled to live in such a dull home, we cannot but see how very foolishly he had behaved. He had thrown himself out of a home and a fixed employment; he had given up all prospects of the future heirship, to fall back upon his old idea of a seafaring life.

But, alas for poor Dick! Well might his uncle call him an unstable character, for long before the *Shooting Star* had reached the far-off port for which she was bound, he felt thoroughly disgusted with the new life which he had chosen. The hard work which fell to his share as a ship's boy, the coarse food doled out to him and his messmates, and the hard blows he often received while attempting to learn the duties of a seaman—all these helped to convince him that, if he were unfitted for a mercantile life, he was equally unfit for the much rougher employment upon which he had now entered.

He had been most unfortunate in his choice of a ship; it was a bad, ill-found vessel, with a wicked master and a reckless crew, and poor Dick did not improve in his new circumstances. We have said that he was easily led to evil, and there were men on board who were quite ready to tempt him to sin. It was a miserable voyage altogether, and long before it was ended his thoughts were running upon this question, 'What was he now to do?' He had signed the ship's articles and was bound for a certain length of time to remain with the *Shooting Star*. But what of that? The lad who had broken the agreement with his uncle would not scruple to break his engagement with the captain of the

Shooting Star. The life was utterly distasteful to him, and he was fully resolved to escape from it if he could. The opportunity soon presented itself. When his vessel arrived in port, and all was bustle and confusion, Dick Charlton, together with three comrades, contrived to get on shore without suspicion, and, diving into the slums of Melbourne, they contrived to hide themselves until the *Shooting Star* had again sailed for the old country.

Poor Dick Charlton! all his young life he had spurned the idea of being under the control of any one; he had longed to be his own master, and to be free to do as he pleased. He was free now, but what was he going to do with his freedom? Alas! before our story has been told, we shall see how terribly Dick fell, and how great were his sufferings.

CHAPTER IV

BROTHER AND SISTER

But all this time we have nearly forgotten our school-girl, Laura Charlton, with whom this story began. To say that this girl, though the youngest member of the family, felt her father's death, with all the sad circumstances which attended it, more than did any of the others, would be quite true; but it must not therefore be supposed that Laura was a more affectionate child than the others, and was grieving over the sad thought that she would never see her father again in this world, for this was not at all Laura's disposition. In truth she was a very strange girl, and, for her age, a very ambitious one. She knew that she was very pretty, and thought that she was very clever, and with her beauty and her talent she had been most anxious for her father's return from India, so that she might secure all the advantages which a residence in London would afford.

She despised the old-fashioned Scottish town where her lot had been cast; she had no great love for her sister Winifred, whose self-denying, kindly disposition seemed to her to be positive weakness. Being the youngest of the family she had been greatly indulged, and, as usually happens in such cases, she had lost much of the respect for her mother which children ought certainly to feel for a parent. Since her father's sad and sudden death, Laura had suffered from a feeling of mortification little suspected by the rest of the family. She remembered how she had boasted at school of her father's return home, of the removal to London, of the possible gay doings there, and school had, for a time at least, become quite distasteful to her, as she imagined she saw in the faces of her young companions a compassionate pity which to the proud girl was hateful indeed. But after a few weeks a change came over her feelings, and she began to study with a diligence which surprised every one. The truth was that Laura had formed a plan for her future life. She knew that the family were now poor, so very poor that possibly on her mother's death there would be no provision for her or her sister. What a terrible position to be in!

But Laura was resolved to avoid any such trouble. She made up her mind that, since she must remain at St. Andrews for the present, she would study hard, secure as good an education as she could, and then, as soon as possible, turn her back upon the hateful place, and secure a position for herself as governess in some high family, where she might see a little of the gay world. This was Laura's plan for her future life; not a bad plan by any means, if her motive had been to earn independence for herself, relieve her mother of the cost of her maintenance, and perhaps be able to add a little to her mother's comforts as she grew older, and became less able to bear the burden of poverty. But thoughts such as these never occurred to Laura. Like her brother Dick, her first thought had always been for self. Between her and her brother Dandie there was almost continual war, the lad, who loved his mother fondly, being vexed and almost shocked by his sister's petulance and indifference to the poor lady's comfort; while Laura, after rudely telling him to mind his own concerns and leave her alone, had sent a shaft flying at him one day which had deeply wounded his feelings.

'If you are so much concerned about mother,' she had said, 'why do you not get some situation for yourself, instead of living on here and adding to her expenses?' Nothing could have been more unkind, or, indeed, more unjust, than a question such as this; for Laura knew quite well that Dandie had been doing his very best to get well-paid employment for himself, although he had not yet succeeded. She knew, too, that his distress at his enforced idleness had been so great that he had actually begun to dispense with many things which hitherto had seemed almost necessaries of life to him. He would eat no butter with his bread; he refused even an egg at breakfast, saying, when his mother expostulated with him on the subject, 'No, no, mother; I am strong and healthy. Many men, who have made their mark in the world, have lived in their youth upon little more than bread and water. I shall eat both eggs and butter with a very good appetite, I do assure you, whenever I can earn them for myself, but not till then.' And with this answer his mother was forced to be content.

But not so Winifred. She could not bear to see her favourite brother actually stinting himself of food. It grieved her more than Dandie knew, though brother and sister kept very few secrets from each other. Some things, of course, Winnie could not tell him if she valued his happiness, which she most truly did. She could not tell him how much she regretted that she had no time to attend school, or even to study at home, and how often she felt the responsibility of household matters almost too much for her, while at the same time she could not cast them upon her mother, whose nervous, anxious constitution quite unfitted her for any burden which her loving daughter could keep from her. On that day, however, when Laura had made the unkind and unsisterly attack upon Dandie which has already been recorded, Winnie and her brother had a long conversation, which resulted in drawing them still nearer in affection the one to the other, and making the burdens of life seem less hard to bear.

Dandie, wandering aimlessly about the house and garden, had opened the door of the morning-room, where he found Winifred seated at the table darning the household linen.

'Winnie,' he said, 'it is a lovely morning, and I am sure a long walk would be good for you. Come with me to the Eagle's Cliff; I want to consult you about something very important. Do come, dear Winnie, as a favour to me.'

And Winnie, hearing these words, immediately laid aside her self-imposed task, and in a very few minutes was ready to accompany her brother to the Eagle's Cliff. But Dandie did not seem to be very ready to speak. He walked along in moody silence, which Winifred did not attempt to break, feeling that it would be best to let him say what he had to say in his own time and way.

At last Dandie spoke, and rather abruptly, too.

'Winnie,' he said, 'I hate to see you so overtaxed as you are. Why does Laura not help you with the needlework? She is surely a very selfish girl. And why does she sit so seldom in the room with the rest of us? Why, we scarcely see her except at meals.'

'Laura is studying very hard, Dandie,' replied Winifred, gently. 'She has begun German, and I am sure you must hear her at the piano before seven in the morning; she practises two hours every day. I wish I could do so too,' she added with a sigh; 'but it is quite impossible, I have so much to do. But please do not look so sorrowful, dear, for I have quite made up my mind that, for the present at least, patching and darning, helping in the store-room and kitchen, is my duty; and, Dandie, the thought that I am relieving poor dear mother of these things makes them easy to me. Now that we have only one servant, we could never get along unless I gave her some assistance. Perhaps you do not know,' she added, laughing a little by way of cheering him up, for she saw a cloud upon his brow; 'perhaps you do not know that those delicious puddings which mother likes so much are all made by me? And that veal pie which you condescended to praise, do you suppose that Sally could have made it? No, Mr. Dandie, the artist is beside you,' and she linked her arm affectionately in his. 'Oh, you don't know what a genius you have for a sister!' she added, as he did not answer, but continued to look gloomily out to the ocean, whose turbulent waters seemed as restless as his own heart.

'I don't know whether you are a genius or not, Winnie,' he said at length (and if Winifred had looked very closely in his face she might have seen bright tears in his eyes), 'but I know that I have a very kind, unselfish girl for my sister; and I know that if it were not for you, Winnie, I think I would——' Here he paused for a minute or two.

'You would do what?' inquired his sister, with an anxious look in her eyes. 'Don't do anything rash, Dandie dear,' she added. 'Remember poor Dick.'

'Yes, Dick has behaved foolishly enough,' said

the lad, bitterly, 'and badly enough too: but at least he is not living idly at home, and eating bread which he has not earned. Winifred, if it were not for you I believe I should enlist as a common soldier.'

But Winifred uttered a cry of dismay. 'Oh, Dandie, brother! and break mother's heart and mine too! But you are not in earnest, you could not be so cruel. Why cannot you have a little patience, dear? Something will certainly turn up for you yet.'

'Winnie, I should not have said what I did,' replied Dandie, 'for in truth I have no thought of enlisting. I will tell you what I mean to do, and I hope you will think my plan is a good one. We have another uncle, Winnie, our father's brother. Don't you remember that mother told us so? Well, I mean to write to him and ask him if he will help me to some employment.'

'And why not?' said Winnie, in a tone of encouragement. 'I would not have liked you to ask him for money; but even though he were estranged from our father, he will surely not refuse to do some small kindness to his children. Is he a married man, Dandie?'

'I don't remember that mother said anything as to that. But why do you ask, Winifred?'

'Because,' she replied, ' if he has a family of his own to place out in the world he might not be able to do anything for you—his own sons would have to be considered first. But are you going to tell mother about this?'

'No,' said Dandie; 'she might see difficulties, and my mind is quite made up to try my uncle. I have failed in every other application I have made, and something else must be tried, or I shall become quite desperate.'

Winnie pressed his hand. 'Never despair, Dandie. Both you and I should remember the motto, "Trust in God, and do the right." Come home now, and I will help you to compose the letter.'

A great weight was lifted off Dandie's heart by this loving converse with his sister; he felt much brighter, and much more able to begin with vigour his efforts after success in life! And yet Winnie could not know any better than he did what was the best plan for him to pursue. She could not really assist him in any one thing, or advance his prospects in the smallest degree; but he felt that her fullest sympathies were his, he felt that whether his new venture was to be a success or a failure he could equally count upon her affectionate

'NEVER DESPAIR, DANDIE.'

interest and friendship. And do our young readers, whether boys or girls, think that this was a small matter, that it would not signify whether a sister or a brother sympathized with them or not? Let any such young people wait for a few years, till the difficulties of life begin to thicken around them, and they will then discover that nothing (save the consolations of religion) helps us more at such sad times than the thought that one human heart beats truly for us, and can love us equally well whether we sink or swim in the struggle that one way or another comes to every one of us. And if it should happen that this dear sympathizer is one who shared the same nursery with us and looked up into the same kind mother's face, surely the happiness which we experience in their loving friendship must be all the greater!

Assuredly Dandie found this to be the case as he sat writing the important letter to his Uncle Charlton, with Winnie looking over his shoulder, and adding now and again her gentle word of advice. And did not the kind sister feel rewarded when she saw how her brother, older and wiser than she was, yet leant upon her for counsel and sympathy? Young girls—you who are so much occupied with your own petty affairs that you have no thought to give to a brother and his troubles—oh, take care lest you thoughtlessly let slip that priceless affection which, if you be able to retain it, may prove the solace of your whole after-life!

But to return to Dandie. We can easily imagine how anxiously both brother and sister watched for an answer to the letter which had been sent to Mr. Charlton. But the answer did come at last, and meanwhile we shall take a peep at Uncle Charlton, and find out why he was so unkind as to leave poor Dandie's letter unanswered for three long weeks.

CHAPTER V

DANDIE SEEKS HIS FORTUNE

Mr. Frederick Charlton was a bachelor uncle, with no fixed place of residence, though he was generally to be found at his club in one of the West-end streets of London. He was seated there one morning in the merry month of May, eating his breakfast and looking over a newspaper, when a servant placed in his hands the letter which had caused so much anxious consideration to Dandie and his sister.

Uncle Charlton read it with a perplexed expression of face as he gathered from its perusal the terrible fact that his unknown nephew intended leaning upon him for advice or assistance of some kind to enable him to fight the battle of life. This was not a pleasant idea to him; he was a selfish, careless fellow; here was a boy of seventeen writing to plague and torment him with his trumpery affairs! It really seemed too bad to Mr. Fred Charlton.

He folded up the letter and began to consider matters.

'Well,' said he to himself, 'the young dog at least does not ask for money; just as well, perhaps, as I can scarcely find enough for myself. What a fool my brother was to make such a marriage, or, indeed, to marry at all! Thank heaven I never tied myself to any woman!' Then as a kindlier thought passed through his mind, a thought of the olden time when he and his brother were boys together, he again took up the letter. 'Not badly expressed,' thought he, 'and after all, the poor lad only asks for work; but why ask me for it? I never found any employment for myself; but stay!' .... Here a bright thought seemed to strike him; he opened his pocket-book, and taking from it another letter written on thin foreign paper, he read it attentively. 'Just the very thing,' said he to himself, 'it will suit my nephew amazingly well; but perhaps I should write to the Count first, and hear all particulars about the situation, before answering the young fellow's letter.'

Well, Uncle Charlton wrote to the Count, and after a few days' delay the Count replied to him.

And now would our young readers like to hear all about it? Would they like to know who the

Count was, and what connection there could be between a Polish nobleman and Dandie Charlton? Well, to understand this we must, as the children say, 'begin at the very beginning,' say a few words first about Poland, and then about Count Demetrius Slavonski, the correspondent of Uncle Charlton.

Most young people are familiar with the story of unhappy Poland, which is far too long to be written here, but still a little of it must be told if we are to understand the position of the Poles at the time of which we write.

It will be enough, however, to say that when Poland, once strong and powerful, had become from various causes too weak to hold her own among the several European nations, she took the fatal step of depending upon Russia for assistance. As well might a lamb ask a wolf for help. From this time began her decline and fall. This was about the year 1717, when Peter the Great occupied the throne of Russia. The Czar Peter sent troops to Poland by way of assisting her against her enemies, but he refused to remove these troops again when they were no longer wanted. By his scheming also the Polish army was greatly reduced, and the country further weakened by internal dissensions. Things went on from bad to worse till 1772, when what was called the first partition of Poland took place, Russia, Prussia, and Austria dividing a large portion of the unhappy country amongst themselves. The Polish people, now aroused to a sense of their terrible position, fought desperately for freedom under 'Kosciusko' and Joseph Poniatowski, the two great and noble-minded Polish patriots whose names should be held in reverence by all who value freedom. Of these two men we shall have something to say further on, at present it is enough to tell that their efforts were all in vain. A second partition of that unhappy country took place (1793), when Russia and Prussia again wrenched away large portions of the country, and two years later a third and last partition took place, the Poles being left without a country, and forced to submit to the iron rule of those who had conquered them. But they did not submit quietly; who could expect it of them? From time to time they rose in rebellion, especially those of them who were under the thraldom of Russia, but never being strong enough to hold their own, these rebellions only brought down sorer suffering upon themselves. They were massacred by the Russian troops, often in cold blood, while many of them who were merely suspected of favouring revolution were torn away from their homes and families, and sent to linger out their lives in the frozen wilds of Siberia.

Early in the present century the hopes of the Polish people were greatly revived by the successes of the French against Russia, and Napoleon having proposed to reconstitute their country (1800), a Polish army joined the French and did good service against Russia in many a hardly contested battle; but Napoleon, instead of keeping his promise to the Poles (which, perhaps, he was not able to do), handed them over to their enemies by the treaty of Tilsit, 1807. Notwithstanding all this, when the French Emperor invaded Russia (1812), he was accompanied by a large army of Poles, and among the many thousands of poor soldiers who perished of cold and hunger during the disastrous retreat of the French were many brave and gallant Poles, who, perhaps, were happier dying thus than living as unwilling slaves to Russia in a land which had once been their own.

It would be a long task even to name the many revolutions which took place after this. We must pass on to the year 1862, when a fresh revolt occurred, followed by terrible reprisals on the part of Russia. So cruel was the treatment of the Poles at this time, that the various governments of

Europe remonstrated with the Czar of Russia, but all in vain. Tumult and murder were everywhere; the wealthier Poles were ruined by fines and confiscations of their property, and of some villages the whole population was put to the sword. It was, indeed, a reign of terror; but at length the exhausted Poles could do no more; the Czar succeeded in trampling out the last embers of insurrection. Men, women, and even children, were executed in great numbers, while crowds were transported to Siberia. After this tranquillity reigned, but it was the tranquillity of the desert.

During this sad period, Count Demetrius Slavonski, the correspondent of Uncle Charlton, was living quietly upon his own estates with the Countess and his only son—a very fine and promising young man.

On account of advancing years and infirmities the old Count had taken no part in the insurrection of his countrymen, though his sympathies had been with them, and he had secretly aided them with money to the extent of his power. But though the old man had remained quietly at home during all these troubles, his son, Count Emile, had not done so. Burning with indignation at the tyranny of Russia and the sufferings of his countrymen, the young man had so compromised himself, that he was seized by the Russians, and, by way of punishment, had been forced into the ranks of the army, and sent to serve as a private in the Caucasus with the regiment of Astrachan. For twenty miserable months he had been there, enduring the utmost misery that a cruel despotism could inflict upon him. But it is not with the young Count that we have to do just now; we shall narrate his sufferings afterwards, and his marvellous escape from the hands of his enemies. At present we must return to the old, sombre, gloomy mansion-house, near Warsaw, where Count Demetrius lived, with the beautiful and stately lady his wife, who, under a quiet and composed manner, concealed a brave and resolute heart, which, alas! was almost broken by the sad fate of her only son.

During his young days, Count Demetrius had spent twelve happy months in England—the land of the free—and had been greatly impressed with all that he had seen there: the cheerful bearing especially of the people, so unlike the down-trodden looks of his unhappy countrymen. During this happy visit to England he had made the acquaintance of Uncle Charlton, and though the two men were singularly unlike in character, they met often, and became mutually attached to each other, so much so, that when the Count returned to Poland, many letters passed between him and his English friend, who, on his part (selfish as we have seen him to be), retained a warm regard for the Polish Count who had visited him in London many years before. After the sad banishment of his only son Emile to the Caucasus, Count Demetrius had fallen into a condition of profound melancholy, from which no one seemed able to rouse him; he wandered aimlessly about the gloomy, neglected gardens and shrubberies which surrounded his mansion, thinking always of the dear absent son who had been as the very light of his eyes when he had lived in his ancestral home with the father and mother who loved him so well.

At length, unable any longer to bear the quiet and desolation of his home, the Count fell upon a somewhat strange plan to create an interest in life for himself; he resolved to take into his family some young man—English if possible—of good birth and education, who could assist him with his books, act as secretary, and read aloud in the evening. All this would help to pass away the time which often hung heavily on the old Count's hands. The more he thought of this the brighter seemed the idea, till at length, with the full concurrence of the Countess, who rejoiced to see her husband taking a cheerful view of anything, a letter was written to Mr. Charlton, asking him to look out for some youth who would be contented to live in the gloomy seclusion of the Count's country house, where he would be well treated and receive a moderate salary; he would also get plenty of fishing and shooting.

'Indeed,' added the poor Count, in his letter to Mr. Charlton, 'I shall feel so glad to see a young face once more beneath my roof, that I shall treat the young man, whoever he may be, quite as well as if he were my own son.'

When Uncle Charlton received this letter from his old friend it rather worried him; he knew no young man whom he could venture to send to Poland, it was a commission quite out of his line; but when the Count's letter was followed in a few days by the earnest appeal from poor Dandie, then Uncle Charlton began to see his way. He would offer the post to his nephew. If he accepted it, as he surely would be glad to do, then the lad was provided for, while at the same time he knew that the Count would be more than pleased to receive into his family the nephew of his old English friend.

And now our readers will clearly see the bright prospects which were opening up for Dandie;

perhaps we should not exactly call them very bright, for he could not be the Count's secretary for ever, and what was this temporary engagement to lead to? But at all events, it was a provision for the present, it offered an amusing and interesting variety in his young life; and what lad would not hail with pleasure the prospect of easy occupation, kind treatment, and leisure for fishing and shooting in a new and interesting country? Certainly these things were not without their charms for our young hero, and it was with a heart beating high with pleasurable expectation, that, after receiving the long-expected letter from Uncle Charlton, he went to lay it before his mother and Winnie, who, though deeply distressed at the idea of parting with him for such an unknown world as Poland seemed to be, yet could not in their present straitened circumstances advise him to remain at home.

'But oh, dear Dandie!' said the loving Winnie, when she thoroughly realized that she must let her brother go, 'do not run into any danger, remember it is a disturbed country, give no offence to any one, and do write often, for how much we shall miss you I can never tell, especially now when so much uncertainty hangs over poor Dick, dear boy! Shall we ever hear of him again?'

CHAPTER VI

IN A FAR COUNTRY

It will be remembered that when Dick Charlton left the ship *Shooting Star* at Melbourne, he was accompanied in his flight by three messmates, who also had made up their minds to try their fortune on land and in a strange country, being all of a roving disposition and sick of a seafaring life, with its hard work and poor pay. Two of these young men were brothers named William and Samuel Turton; what had attracted Dick to such companions it would be hard to say, for they were both very rough and ignorant lads; but his fancy for the third young seaman is more easily explained, for Frank Devon was a quiet lad, better educated than the others, and therefore more of a companion. He had also been very helpful to Dick, whose arm had been broken at an early period of the voyage, a misfortune which the captain and mate had resented by unlimited bad language and hard blows.

Such were the four young men, who, having abandoned their ship, were now hanging about Melbourne, without any money or any certain employment. Finding that this state of matters could not last long, Dick and his companions resolved to travel on foot towards the Kajunga diggings, which at this time were beginning to attract attention, trusting to chance to supply them with food and the necessary outfit of diggers for the precious metal. And they were more fortunate than they deserved to be, for having reached a bush station whose owner had been deserted by most of his men during the first days of harvest, they found ample and well-paid employment for nearly three weeks; indeed the settler, highly pleased with Dick and Frank Devon, would fain have engaged these two to remain with him had they been willing to do so, but the fever of restlessness was upon them both, and they would not stay. Had poor Dick accepted this offer and begun an honest and industrious life, all might yet have been well with him; but thoughtless and perverse as ever he put the chance away from him, and with the wages earned he supplied himself with an outfit, and accompanied by the other three lads pursued the road to Kajunga. Upon their experience and adventures at the diggings we do not mean to enter, it was that of many other men, who, arriving in full expectation of making a fortune in a very short time, yet found themselves after a month or two as penniless as when they first stepped upon the gold-field, and with many another bitter experience besides.

It was a life of great excitement and feverish exhaustion, and such a life men find it hard to live without some stimulus for their flagging energies, and this they sought in drink. Therefore as soon as half-a-dozen men had settled themselves down in any particular locality, immediately a grog-shop was started by some one, who left others to dig the gold, being well aware that if he kept a plentiful supply of tempting liquors, most of the precious metal would, sooner or later, flow into his till. And so it was; for the recklessness of the poor gold-diggers was almost beyond belief; instead of saving up what they obtained so as to enable them to start in some better way of life, each one of them seemed to desire nothing better than to throw it away again, and what better opportunity could they have than the grog-shop presented?

So at least thought Dick Charlton and his three companions, who were very constant customers there, for by this time Dick had thrown off all the restraints which had hitherto bound him, and was as reckless of consequences as any of his less educated friends. And did he never think of his home in all these terrible months of riot and dissipation? Did he never remember his widowed mother and young sister, who ceaselessly prayed for the poor wanderer, each day hoping that a letter might come to tell them where he was, and how he was living? Yes, Dick did remember these dear ones, for, though thoughtless and selfish, he was not entirely bad—few men are; but the remembrance of his home was a constant pain to him; he felt how sadly he had fallen, and he loathed himself for the life he was leading, yet he would not give it up, he put away from him the repentant thought, and plunged yet deeper into the vortex of sin. At length an event took place which exercised a great influence over the future life of Dick Charlton.

We all know that drinking leads to quarrelling and fighting, even among friends, for when men and lads are heated by wine or spirits, when passion is furiously excited, they do not wait to consider who is a friend or who is a foe, and so it came about that one Saturday night, when Dick and his companions were as usual drinking in the wooden shanty which served as a public-house, a fierce quarrel arose between Dick and Frank Devon, who in their sober hours were the best of friends.

The quarrel was about such a trifling matter that the next day on thinking it over Dick could not remember what had been the difficulty between him and his companion, but it had been attended by awful results. In the heat of dispute and maddened by the drink he had swallowed, Frank struck a blow at his friend, an insult which Dick resented by knocking his assailant down, amid the cheers of the revellers who were seated beside them, and who started up that they might form a ring for a regular stand-up fight. But the stand-up fight never took place; Frank Devon, who by the blow from his friend had been hurled amid a heap of old iron, still lay upon the ground, pale and insensible. The others, seeing this, gathered round the fallen man, endeavouring to rouse him, so that they might not be defrauded of the expected fight; but every effort was in vain, the unfortunate youth never moved again, his neck having been broken by the fall.

That awful night Dick Charlton retired to his

tent feeling as though the curse of Cain was upon him; he had slain his friend, the lad who had been kind and attentive to him when he suffered from a broken limb and the taunts and blows of a brutal captain. Frank Devon was dead and gone to his account, and it was his hand which had struck the cruel blow! What did it matter to Dick Charlton that his reckless companions all assured him that no blame could possibly attach to him in the matter, he had only done what most men would do, given blow for blow? The death was an unfortunate accident, nothing more; he was certainly not to blame, especially as he had not been the aggressor, poor Frank having struck the first blow.

This was all very true, and doubtless even in an English Court of Justice such a case could never be considered as a murder; but do our young readers suppose that such thoughts could clear Dick Charlton's conscience from the horrible weight of guilt? No, as he lay that night in his tent, his heart bounding as though it would burst from his bosom, his temples throbbing, and his whole heart filled with the anguish of remorse, poor Dick might have been a warning to other thoughtless lads and men. For would this miserable death have taken place if Dick had been sober? No; he well knew

AN INSULT WHICH DICK RESENTED.

that drink had been the cause of the fatal blow, and now he loathed the very idea of it; yet had there been any spirits beside him at this moment he would certainly have drunk all he could lay his hands on in order to drown the horrible pangs of remorse. Such slaves to the demon of drink can men become.

This terrible affair, and the consequent anguish of mind endured by Dick Charlton, brought on a terrible illness, during which time he was roughly nursed by the storekeeper, who threw down a bundle of wood shavings in a corner as a bed for him, and gave him a can of tea morning and evening, leaving him in other respects to struggle back to life as he best could. And poor Dick, being young and strong, did struggle back to life after a few weeks, and sat thin and shivering, by the camp fire, with bloodshot eyes, and a heart as heavy as lead. Ah, could his mother and Winnie have seen their poor prodigal then!

It was a dismal and depressing story that the storekeeper had to tell him on his recovery from the fever which had prostrated him. There had been a change of luck, so he said. The greater part of the gold seemed to have been worked out, and many of the men had gone away to try some other diggings. One of his two remaining shipmates, Samuel Turton, had been drowned in attempting to cross the creek during a freshet on the river, while his brother, William Turton, had gone off with the others, leaving all his debts unpaid, and without so much as asking how Dick was getting on, or if he was likely to recover or die.

'More fools they to leave,' continued the storekeeper, grumbling. 'There's plenty of gold here yet, as time will show. Meanwhile, I'll not move a step myself, as long as customers come to my bar.'

It is sometimes said that wicked men are at least kind to each other. Well, so far, perhaps, as long as it suits, but it is a friendship scarcely to be relied on, as poor Dick Charlton felt while sitting in the storekeeper's shanty, penniless, weak, and forsaken, and worse than all, with a conscience which goaded him with his evil doings till he almost wished he was dead. All his gold had been seized by the storekeeper, who declared that he had been put to great expense by Dick's unfortunate illness.

'Indeed you owe me more than your gold is worth,' continued the man, whose naturally hard disposition had not been improved by his occupation;

'but as you are cleaned out, and not quite up to the mark yet, you may stay here a day or two longer; but next week you must tramp, well or ill, mind that.'

'Tramp!' echoed poor Dick, bitterly. 'Where to, I wonder?'

'To the devil, if you like,' said the man indifferently; 'it is all one to me; but out of my place you must go.'

That night Dick Charlton lay in his miserable bed pondering over the bitter past. How bitter it was! He could scarcely bear to think of it, scarcely bear to think of his mother and Winnie, whose sad and reproachful faces seemed to haunt his pillow. And yet he knew that even with all his follies and his sins known to them he would be received with open arms if he could only make up his mind to return. But that was what he could not do. He could not go home, penniless and in rags, to live upon his widowed mother. No, he must first redeem the past if ever he was to see those dear ones again. But would he have fortitude and energy enough to redeem the past? Would it not be almost better, at least easier, to continue in future as he had done in the past, live a reckless life, swear, fight, and drown his conscience in drink? Which was it to be?

It was a turning-point in Dick's life, a turning-point such as we all come to at various times and in a variety of ways, when we seem to stand where two roads meet and must choose one or other of the two. It is sometimes said that there is a fate in the choice we make, and that we really cannot help ourselves; but we must not delude ourselves with such an idea. Our wills are free, and on ourselves rests the momentous burden of making a choice between good and evil.

Dick, after much pondering, made his choice on that eventful night, although we do not mean to tell our readers whether he chose the good or the evil. All we shall say at present is this, that his mind being fully made up as to the life he intended to live in the future, he cautiously got out of bed in the dim grey of the early morning, and stole away from the creek where he had endured such misery, once more to try his fortune in the world.

CHAPTER VII

ADVENTURES IN POLAND

We must suppose, before resuming our story, that two long years have passed away, bringing with them some changes to the Charlton family.

Our first interest is with our friend Dandie, who after a two years' residence with Count Demetrius Slavonski became such an admirer of Poland, and felt such warm sympathy for its unfortunate yet heroic people, that he could willingly have spent his whole life among them. This feeling of friendship was shared by the Count, who loved the frank and perfectly trustworthy young Englishman.

Dandie had been, after a time, introduced to several of the Count's personal friends, especially to one, Count Stanislas Praga, an old man who had not been involved in the late insurrection, believing as he did that it was ill-judged and hopeless, and would only serve as a pretext to the Russians to bring down more suffering upon the Polish peasantry. This opinion proved to be a correct one, though it is hard for men while suffering from horrible oppression to be always guided by calmness and common sense in their natural attempts to resist it. Count Praga had been in his younger days an ardent sportsman, and it was to him an intense enjoyment to revive these recollections by taking Dandie under his guidance, and conducting him to the depths of the wild Polish forests where lurked many a wolf, fox, martin, and polecat, the pursuit of which had been one of his chief youthful pleasures.

On one occasion the hospitable old Count invited Dandie to visit him and remain for a week, that he might take part in a projected wolf-hunt, which he had arranged partly to divert the minds of his people from the political troubles in which they had been involved, and partly because one of these animals had been prowling about the mansion, terrifying the peasant women and their children.

Dandie looked forward to this wolf-hunt with great delight, though when the time came he did not find it quite so pleasant an adventure as he had expected. It was mid-winter, and very cold, while a snowstorm was evidently impending. The party engaged in the hunt did not, however, give up their expedition on account of the weather. Rather did they press forward until they were in the heart of the forest. Not having as yet met with any signs of wolves, the party scattered here and there, pursuing any small game which they could find, Dandie and Count Praga remaining together, talking about England, a country in which the Count took the deepest interest. After a time a loud whoop was heard, then the clash of arms, and a loud call for the Count by name.

Count Praga listened attentively for a few minutes, then turned to his companion.

'It is the change of guard,' he said. 'These are the relieving sentries returning to their posts. The insolent curs will be questioning my people, and giving them trouble; I must go to explain matters. Pray wait here till I return.' And so saying, the Count turned into a by-path and quickly disappeared.

Dandie, thus left to himself, began idly to look about him, peering into the brushwood, and starting a polecat, which, however, he did not pursue, the Count having asked him to remain where he was. Presently, however, the long-expected snow began to fall; it grew ominously dark, and a low, moaning wind began to sweep through the forest. Dandie regarded these changes with some anxiety, especially as he observed that the thickly-falling snow was speedily obliterating all traces of the footpath by which they had entered the forest. And where could the Count be? No sound was to be heard from the direction in which he had gone; silence reigned all around. It was not a pleasant position for one who was quite ignorant of forest work, and very naturally afraid of losing himself in such a desolate region. After some thought Dandie resolved to retrace his steps without waiting for the Count, and get back to the mansion as quickly as possible. Easier said than done; the path had now become quite covered, and Dandie had not gone far before he found that he had hopelessly lost himself. But the sky was clearing; through the leafless boughs of the forest he could discern the stars, and he knew from them how he should direct his course. He therefore pushed on steadily, and tried to keep up his courage.

'I shall find my way now,' he said to himself, 'path or no path. Patience is all that is wanted, so here goes.'

But what was this he saw on the ground right in front of him—a something that made his heart leap into his mouth? Wolf-tracks, fresh trodden, were printed on the newly-fallen snow. Dandie had been following up the trail; the animal might be—nay, must be—lurking in one of the surrounding thick bushy coverts, and might at any moment spring out upon him unawares. Poor Dandie! he felt that his life at that moment was not worth a groat. A rustling in the thicket behind him now alarmed him dreadfully, and he swung himself up into the branches of a tree, and crouched there unhurt at a safe distance from the ground. And not a moment too soon, for the wolf was already prowling about below, a gaunt, strong, savage animal, looking up at him, and howling round and round the tree. Dandie was in a trap. He soon began to feel how small was the chance of the creature tiring of its watch or abandoning it before daylight. There might be a pack of them hanging about, which might come and imprison him there till—when?

All at once a new danger presented itself. The drifted snow was falling upon him from the boughs above, and he felt a chill numbness creeping through his veins, and a strange drowsiness overpowering him. Then he knew that the worst had come. If he fell from the tree he would fall into the very jaws of the wolf below. At this moment, however, he heard, to his inexpressible relief of mind, the hum of voices and the crackling of brushwood—his friends were returning. And in less time than it takes to write about it the monstrous grey wolf lay dead at the feet of Count Praga, who was assisting his young English friend to descend from the tree, while half-a-dozen sturdy peasants dressed in sheepskin were already skinning the monster and cutting off its paws.

'How can I sufficiently apologize for my prolonged absence?' said the Count; 'but if you could know all the annoyance I have had at the hands of those dogs of Russians! However, let it pass. After a change of clothing and a good dinner you will feel all right again. So come along, my young friend, our next wolf-hunt I hope may be a pleasanter one.'

Dandie Charlton at this time stood a great chance of being fairly spoiled by kindness; the servants one and all were ready to do his pleasure, while Count Demetrius himself seemed only to be happy when he had the young Englishman at hand. His duties were very light, indeed almost nominal; he acted as librarian (the Count loved reading, and possessed many valuable books in various European languages), he wrote letters for his patron, walked out with him through the rather gloomy and neglected grounds that surrounded the mansion, and read aloud to him in the evenings. Long before the end of the two years he had been made acquainted with many details of the Polish insurrection, and with much of the Count's own family history, and that of his son, the young Count Emile, who seemed never to be entirely absent from his father's thoughts for a single hour. He had also read with the Count much of the history of Poland during the trying period when it had been partitioned among its enemies, and he could sympathize with the old man in his indignation at Russia and Prussia. What interested Dandie most during these readings and conversations with the old Count was the character and the prowess of Kosciusko and Joseph Poniatowski, the two celebrated Polish patriots. A little information about these men may perhaps be interesting.

Kosciusko, who was descended from an ancient and honourable though poor family, had been born about the middle of last century. He had gone to America, and served in the War of Independence there, but he returned to Poland while still a young man, and in the terrible conflicts with Russia, which preceded the second partition of the country, he soon showed his own nation, and Russia, too, what stuff he was made of. One instance may be given. It was necessary to hold a certain position against the Russians for as long a time as possible, and to Kosciusko was appointed this duty. It was not an easy task, the place was in a ruinous condition, and he had only twenty-four hours in which to fortify it; then he had only four thousand men, while the Russians numbered no less than sixteen thousand; yet he held the position for five days, long enough to do great damage to the Russians, who were thus detained from further advance, while the Poles had a breathing time in which to assemble themselves in numbers.

This brilliant feat of arms laid the foundation of Kosciusko's military reputation, but it was of no avail to save his country from its fate, for this insurrection of the Poles was almost immediately followed by the second partition of their country of which we have already written.

Again in 1794, shortly before the third and last partition of the country, Kosciusko put himself at the head of a new rebellion, and with only twenty thousand regular troops and about as many ill-armed peasants, he resisted for months the united Russian and Prussian army of a hundred and fifty thousand men. Many tempting proposals were made to him by the Prussian King, but the patriot resented them all. At last he was overpowered in battle, and fell from his horse covered with wounds, only uttering these sad and foreboding words, *Finis Poloniæ.*

Happy would it have been for Kosciusko had he died on that battlefield, for he would have been spared all knowledge of the final fate of his country; but he recovered from his terrible wounds, and languished in a Russian prison till the accession of the Emperor Paul, who restored him to freedom, and handed to him his sword. But Kosciusko refused to receive it, saying, 'I do not need a sword when I have no longer a country.' He then retired to France, where he spent the remainder of his days, his body being carried back to his beloved Poland, and buried at Cracow, where so many patriots lie.

Joseph Poniatowski was a man of the same stamp as Kosciusko, and lived during the same terrible times, but his career was even more glorious and eventful than that of his friend. We have not space here to enter into details as to his life. It was full of patriotic endeavours for the benefit of his countrymen, and when these all failed, then, burning with hatred of the Russians, he joined

Napoleon with a large army of Poles in the attempted invasion of Russia. We all know how this failed, and how Napoleon (who left thousands of his poor soldiers dead of cold and hunger on the frozen plains of Russia) once more gathered an army and attempted to regain his lost position. Then followed the battle of Leipsic, where Poniatowski once more took his place on the side of France. Again Napoleon was defeated, and Poniatowski, being compelled to retreat, was drowned in attempting to cross a river. His body was recovered six days later, embalmed, and sent to Cracow, where it was placed beside the body of Kosciusko his friend.

CHAPTER VIII

FLIGHT AND RESCUE

But we must now return to Dandie Charlton. During the first few months that he spent at the house of Count Demetrius Slavonski, he had often observed that the Countess looked fixedly and almost anxiously in his face, while her husband talked so freely as he did of Poland and of his absent son. The poor lady seemed anxious to stop these revelations; she evidently half distrusted the young foreigner, English though he might be, and would have liked to persuade the Count to greater reticence of speech.

Count Demetrius was a man of a naturally open and kindly disposition, greatly beloved by the peasantry on his estates, to whom he was always considerate and kind. But he was imprudent, even to rashness, and it was well for him that Dandie was not only trustworthy, but so discreet and so thoroughly interested in the family that every communication made to him was a secret faithfully kept in his own bosom. Not even to his mother or to Winnie did he retail a single piece of the information received from the Count. To them he merely narrated his impressions of the country, his fishing and shooting expeditions, and the pleasure he felt in being useful to such kind and good friends. His letters, when they arrived at the Priory, were a great source of delight to Mrs. Charlton and Winnie, and to Laura also, for she, poor girl, now took a deep interest in Dandie and his affairs. An affliction of a severe kind had proved a blessing in disguise to Laura, had taught her the evil of selfishness, and brought her into friendlier relations with the other members of the family.

Poor Laura for nearly a year had been shut up a prisoner in her own room, with but small prospect of ever being able to leave it again. She had fallen on the ice during a severe winter, the first after Dandie left home, and had so seriously injured her back that she had never since been able to put her foot to the ground. How terrible this affliction was to the proud and ambitious young girl we can easily imagine. What days of fretting and nights of weeping before she became at all reconciled to the sad position in which she found herself, and could appreciate in some small degree the loving patience of Winnie, who waited upon her sick and suffering sister with the utmost devotion. It was during these sad days that Dandie's amusing and interesting letters became such a delight to Laura and a pleasant variety in her sad life.

But we must return to Poland, and we must bear in mind that two years have passed away, two years which have thoroughly established Dandie in the good graces not only of the master of the household, but of the lady Countess, his wife. It was winter-time, the long, cold winter of Poland, when on one occasion the Count, who seemed nervous and oppressed since morning, thus addressed his young secretary—

'We shall not have any reading this evening,' he said. 'I feel restless and ill at ease; it is stormy too, and snow seems to be impending. On such gloomy days as this my mind invariably turns to my unhappy son! Where is he now? What is he doing? What is he enduring among the enemies of his country? Ah, if I could but lift the veil which conceals him from me! Could I but assure myself that he is well, that he does not suffer! but how could that be? Could my Emile be an enforced soldier in the ranks of the Czar and not suffer? Impossible!' And the poor father rose and walked to the window, where he sadly watched the great flakes of snow which were already beginning to fall.

Count Demetrius little knew what an eventful day this was to be; he little knew that his poor Emile had already fled from the misery of his position, and was at this very minute struggling through terrible difficulties in the almost hopeless attempt to reach once more his happy childhood's home! But before narrating the events of that evening we must go back a little, and see something of Emile's life in the Caucasus in the midst of his country's enemies.

For nearly three years now this unhappy youth had been enduring the utmost misery which a cruel despotism could inflict upon him. It was not merely privation which he had to suffer, but studied insults and unjust punishments, inflicted with the deliberate intention of breaking his spirit and crushing his heart. He had fought and marched with his half-savage comrades in arms, had endured the hardest details of a hard life with uncomplaining courage and noble pride, upheld by the stern resolution that he would not allow his bitter enemies to know how much they made him suffer. But another humiliation was in store for him: he was made a servant to a Russian major.

This man, who was a cruel coward, detested by all his subordinates, treated the young exile in the most barbarous manner, mocking his country and his creed, and making every duty he had to perform as bitter and odious as a petty despot could do. Still the young Pole suffered in silence, till one day the Russian struck him across the face with a cane. The next moment the Major lay grovelling in the dust screaming for help, having been struck down by a blow from the outraged youth, who immediately turned and fled. But where could he go? A Pole, a deserter, penniless, and on foot, with hundreds of miles of dreary morass and gloomy forest between him and his home, surely he might as well give himself up to his enemies and die. But no, life was precious, and worth an effort. Youth, courage, and hope were all his, and to that dear though far-distant home he resolved to fly, or perish in the attempt.

It would occupy too much space to detail all that he suffered during the terrible wanderings he now had to endure, hiding in the woods day by day, and travelling by night, at times fed and sheltered by some poor serf who pitied his forlorn condition, at other times hunted down by the peasantry in hopes of reward. He succeeded in changing clothes with a peasant, who gave him a sheepskin cloak for his uniform, but this did not save him from being pursued by a troop of Cossacks, who nearly overtook him, when he leaped into a river and swam across. But, alas! a rifle-ball wounded him in the arm as he was scrambling up the bank on the other side. Had the soldiers followed him at this dreadful moment he must inevitably have fallen into their hands, but they came no further, and faint, drenched, and bleeding, he pursued his desperate way until at length he arrived in the immediate neighbourhood of his home, apparently only to die. But he was not to die. A mother's brave and resolute heart, able to dare anything for the sake of those she loved, was to be made happy by being able to rescue from the grave her only and beloved son.

Now we return to that evening when Count Demetrius seemed so nervous and ill at ease.

The family had retired for the night, all but the Countess, who, brooding over her son's fate, was often in the habit of sitting up long after others were asleep, when she was free to indulge her sorrow. On this evening she was gazing out of her chamber window into the quiet garden and the dark forest beyond, when a wan and haggard figure, dressed in tattered sheepskin, emerged from the wood, and gazed up to the windows of the mansion. Miserably changed as he was, none except his mother could have recognized him, but her eyes could not be deceived. She knew that gaunt figure to be her son, her own Emile; but so unexpected was the sight that for a few minutes she imagined that he must have died far away, and that his shadow had come to warn her that they would meet on earth no more. But presently her strong mind rejected this idea, and lighting her lamp with a trembling hand, she glided downstairs and passed out into the shrubbery.

It was, indeed, her poor boy, but already he had fallen to the ground, faint, bleeding, and, as she thought, dying. The poor mother dared not bring the sufferer into his own father's house, for some of the household servants, one especially, were not entirely to be trusted. Even the Count himself, were he to learn the truth about his son, would certainly with his nervous temperament betray the fugitive from sheer anxiety not to do so.

To whom could she turn in this terrible emergency? Emile must be fed and attended to immediately, while in a few hours the whole household would be astir. Instantly the thought flashed through her mind, her husband's foreign secretary! Could she entrust the all-important secret to him? True, he was very young, and for some time she had looked upon him with suspicion, but she had long since laid aside her doubts regarding him. Besides, he was English, he came from the land of liberty, the land where the meanest were free, and where the coldest heart among them would stir at the recital of sufferings such as her Emile had endured. Yes, she would trust the young Englishman, and gliding softly through the sleeping household, she knocked gently at his door.

How can we picture the astonishment of Dandie when he found the stately Countess Slavonski a suppliant at his feet, imploring him in suppressed but anguished tones to aid her in saving her Emile? His first thought was that she must be dreaming, but on thoroughly understanding the situation his young blood warmed to the task before him, and he declared himself ready to do everything he could to insure the safety of the young Count.

'We have but little time,' replied the lady, in agitated tones. 'Oh, follow me quickly, but make no noise, all my household are not to be trusted!' and Dandie with a beating heart followed silently after his guide.

The poor youth still lay on the ground almost senseless, and half dead with cold; his wounded arm, too, was in a very bad condition for want of proper attention. Dandie lifted him up in his strong young arms, and with the help of the Countess contrived to convey him to an outhouse, over which were two rude chambers intended to accommodate husbandmen, but which had long been empty. Here they hurriedly laid the young Count, and then fetched blankets, food, and wine, while Emile, quite unable to speak, though conscious of his mother's presence and caresses, could only feebly clasp her hand, tears of utter weakness rolling down his cheeks. All unwillingly they had to leave him, for day was breaking and the risk of detection was imminent; but before they went he had sunk into a deep and blessed repose. It was hard for the poor mother to go, to leave her newly restored son, to leave him all alone in a dark outhouse. But it had to be done, and the two conspirators, for such we may call them, glided away, re-entered the mansion, and sought their several chambers.

What a strange episode was this in Dandie's life, and what an opportunity presented itself to him of befriending this interesting family, by assisting the Countess to take care of her unfortunate son! He could scarcely close his eyes, so anxious did he feel to know the events of the morrow.

CHAPTER IX

A RIDE FOR LIFE

WE have said that one servant in especial of the Count's household could scarcely be relied on; this was Louis, the major-domo, a Russo-German by birth. Though the lady could not trust this man, yet she dared not dismiss him. He was an excellent servant, and quite a favourite with the unsuspicious Count. After events proved that the lady's suspicions were well founded, and that Louis was a spy in the pay of the Russian Government.

The day after this night of peril there was great excitement at the house, for a Commissary of Police, accompanied by a party of dragoons, arrived with a mighty clatter, in order to search for and apprehend Emile Slavonski, on the charge of deserting from the army. The servants were rigorously examined, the extensive mansion was searched from garret to cellar, while the official in command tried by artful questions addressed to the Count to draw out some information as to his son's hiding-place. But the Count really knew nothing, while the astonishment he exhibited on hearing of Emile's flight was too genuine to be mistaken, and the police were compelled to believe that the runaway had never reached his father's house.

'He has been starved in the forests,' they said, with a brutal laugh, as they galloped away, none of them having thought it worth while to look over that deserted building where the young Count lay.

Meanwhile the two allies, the mother and the young secretary, were greatly disturbed by this terrible danger so happily overpast for the present, and they both felt that to leave Emile where he was, exposed to chance visits from the servants, was not to be thought of; yet where could he go? What asylum was open to him, proscribed as he was by the Russian Government?

At last the Countess bethought herself of a plan, which she hurriedly communicated to Dandie, entreating him at the same time to be very cautious to maintain as much as possible his usual manner, especially when any of the servants were present. There was, she told him, a lodge in the forest inhabited by a woodman, whose wife had nursed the young Count, and loved him with a foster mother's devotion. These good people were entirely trustworthy, and in their cottage Emile would be as safe as he could be anywhere in Poland; and to this retreat the Countess proposed that they should convey her son.

It was a task fraught with the utmost danger, but what will a mother's love not attempt in order to save the life of an only child? As soon as the young Count could stand, they hurriedly conveyed him at dead of night to the woodman's hut, where they saw him laid in a comfortable bed amid the tears of the kind and faithful old woman who had tended him in his infancy.

But the lodge in the forest could only be a temporary retreat; both the Countess and Dandie felt that it was necessary to get him across the Prussian frontier, and that without delay. Prussia, fortunately, was not far off, but the frontier guards were on the alert, and so were prowling bands of Cossacks; while money, horses, and a suitable disguise, all required to be provided. Terrible difficulties beset them on every hand. Winter had set in with great severity, and the ground was covered with snow, when Dandie set out one morning in a very anxious frame of mind to visit the young Count in the woodman's lodge. He had felt oppressed for several days with terrible anxiety; he felt sure that some of the servants were watching his face whenever he chanced to meet them in the mansion, while the Countess, too, was under the same impression. Emile, too, was growing restless and nearly desperate; he was now almost restored to strength, and the necessity of remaining closely confined to the forest hut almost seemed to suffocate him.

'I must leave this,' he said one morning to Dandie, 'I must leave this; my presence here, if discovered, means confiscation and ruin to my father, and I cannot bear the thought.'

Dandie, who had become much attached to Emile, tried to soothe the young man and to lift him out of this morbid state of mind; but it was not easy, indeed he became infected with it himself, and constantly lived in an atmosphere of apprehension, not knowing what might happen at any moment.

One cold, snowy morning, as we have already said, he had left the castle on a pretended duck-shooting expedition, but in reality to visit Count Emile at the forest lodge. On his way thither, as he passed by an enormous pile of roughly-hewn logs, he became aware that two men were in close conversation on the other side, one of the two being Louis, the major-domo. Dandie bent forward and listened with a pale face and a beating heart. The spy, while stipulating for a large reward, was undertaking to point out the retreat of the young Count, while the other conspirator was to bring forward a band of Cossacks.

The young secretary, filled with consternation, returned to the mansion, and, seeking an interview with the Countess, told her this terrible tale. For a moment the poor mother almost gave way, but she speedily rallied.

'I knew it,' she said; 'I have felt sure of it for days past. Louis has dogged your steps to the forest; my son must fly, and immediately, or he is a dead man; but how—weak as he still is?'

It was a terrible moment for Dandie; he felt that the whole responsibility of this grave matter must lie with him; unless he could come to the front and arrange matters for the young Count, he would be a prisoner in the hands of the Russian police before close of day. Could he do this? No wonder if he hesitated; he was still very young, scarcely twenty, and little experienced as yet in the difficulties of life; besides, the duty which lay before him involved great risk to his own life; if the young Count should be caught, he himself would certainly also be seized as aiding and abetting his escape.

But Dandie Charlton was no common youth; he was kind-hearted, prompt, and sensible, and in half as short a time as it takes to tell it he had made up his mind to venture all.

'I will go with your son,' he said to the Countess; 'I will ride with him to the frontier; it can be done in four hours, and we have a fair start.'

'You!' said the poor lady, for the first time melting into tears; 'you! a stranger, would you sacrifice your young life? Oh, I ought not to allow you! I ought not to accept your noble offer. You are young, my friend, and you, too, have a mother.'

Dandie pressed her hand. 'I must go,' he said, 'and immediately. You, dear madam, will pray for us.'

'Stay,' said the Countess, 'only one moment,' and leaving the room she speedily returned carrying a bag of gold. 'I have kept this,' she said, 'unknown to my husband for emergencies. In our unhappy country emergencies continually arise; take it and use it freely, and go with a mother's grateful blessing.'

As all the men-servants had gone to a wedding in the village, Dandie had the coast clear. He went to the stable, where he hastily saddled two fine horses, and was just leading them out when Louis appeared at the door! Their eyes met, and the traitor saw that his villainy had been discovered.

'Not so fast, Herr Englander,' said he insolently. 'Your pretty pleasure-trip is spoiled,' and he seized the bridle of the nearest horse.

Now Dandie was eminently peaceable, but at this moment he was desperate, and Louis, who little knew the power that lay in an English fist, was speedily knocked down, and lay whining for mercy. Not a moment was to be lost; Dandie bound the wretch's hands together and tied him to a post, then led out the horses and mounted. But the animals did not know him; they pranced and neighed, while to his horror the neigh was answered by other horses far off, followed by the wailing sound of the Cossack trumpet. The Czar's bloodhounds were already on the move and rapidly approaching.

In a few minutes, however, Dandie had reached the lodge, and rapidly told his story.

'Dear friend,' said the poor young Count as he mounted, 'you should not come with me; these Cossacks are wolves when they scent blood and plunder.'

But Dandie wrung his hand. 'We go together,' he said. 'Say no more,' and the two friends rode away at a rapid rate.

Quick as they were, however, they had no sooner emerged from the forest into a region of morass and brushwood than loud shouts behind them caused them to look back. The whole troop of wild riders, about forty in number, were dashing over the heath towards them. Now Emile knew the country well from his earliest boyhood, and his knowledge did him good service in this extremity. He dodged here and there through the broken ground, warily avoiding the treacherous morass into which the Cossacks immediately floundered, thus saving much precious time. But it was a terrible ride, now plunging through banks of snow, now stumbling over rocks and the gnarled roots of trees, till after an hour's hard work they reached smoother ground, and Emile, pale and gasping, pointed with his whip to a low swelling hill not far off. 'You see that hill, my friend,' he said, ' with a white cottage and a flag-staff? That is Prussian ground; once there, we are safe. On, my friend, on,' and away they went like the wind.

But between the fugitives and the frontier was a dark stretch of forest, beyond which water gleamed. There was not only a forest to struggle through, but a river to be forded, while Emile's horse was almost dead-beat. Through the wood they tore, stooping their heads to avoid collision with the snow-laden branches, while the Cossacks, yelling like hounds, came rattling on behind, every now and then sending a bullet whistling through the air, as they were almost within range. The fugitives had reached the river and pulled up; it was not frozen, but rolled on deep and dark.

'We must swim for it,' cried Emile; 'head your horse to that spit of land, it is the only safe point.'

He plunged into the flood followed by Dandie; but the next moment a bullet crashing on its way mortally wounded his horse, which reared and floundered, rolled over, and finally sank; while the Cossacks set up a shout of exultation. Dandie, however, with a pluck which he did not know he possessed, caught hold of Emile by the collar, and contrived to drag him free from the dying horse.

'Save yourself, my friend,' said the poor young Pole, 'and never mind me.'

Dandie had no breath to reply, his own horse was giving him terrible trouble, while with his left hand he was grasping Emile by the hair. Still, hope, which had almost died out of him, again sprung up in his heart; his horse's feet touched the ground, and soon, amid shouts and execrations from the Cossacks, he was urging the panting animal up the slopes on the other side, still dragging Emile along with him.

The Prussian guards, who had been spectators of the exciting chase, now came running out of their huts filled with curiosity and excitement, and actually gave a cheer as the two dripping fugitives reached the flag-staff, and were for the moment safe.

'Your passports, young gentlemen!' they cried. 'What, you have none? Then you are prisoners in the name of his Majesty of Prussia.'

Poor Dandie was in despair, thinking that their dearly bought liberty was about to be rudely wrested from them, but Emile knew better. By a judicious use of his mother's gold pieces he suc-

CONTRIVED TO DRAG HIM FREE FROM THE DYING HORSE.

ceeded in enlisting the sympathies of the Prussian guard, who, after all, had little love for their Russian neighbours. Accordingly, when about half-an-hour afterwards the Cossacks contrived to get over the river, and an officer of Russian police came up to demand, in the Czar's name, the extradition of 'Emile Slavonski,' the Prussian sergeant demurred, talked of writing for instructions to headquarters, and finally refused to give up the fugitives until his head inspector should arrive to decide the point.

Two hours later, having dried their clothes, at least partially, and having been refreshed with a much-needed cup of hot coffee, the two friends were quietly allowed to go, mounted on a peasant's rude cart; and, with much difficulty and not a little bribery, they managed to traverse Prussia and reach Hamburg, where they were perforce compelled to remain for a time, Emile being in a burning fever, and almost delirious. What was to be their next move? What asylum was open to the young Count, penniless as he was, and without even a change of clothing? As for Dandie, he felt as though he were dreaming. A few days ago quietly residing in Poland, with no thought of any immediate change of locality; now on his way home to St. Andrews, for Dandie felt that no other alternative was open to him; he and his poor friend must in the first instance seek a refuge at the Priory, as soon as Emile was sufficiently recovered to leave Hamburg.

Meanwhile, having procured a quiet lodging under feigned names, and persuaded his companion to lie down to rest, he summoned an English doctor, to whom he confided the whole story. Having done this he sat down by Emile's bed and wrote a long letter home.

CHAPTER X

STRANGE TIDINGS

WHEN Dandie's letter reached his home it found the family there in great though pleasurable excitement, for a letter had just been received from Dick, poor wandering Dick, of whom they had heard absolutely nothing since the sad day, now more than two years ago, when he had run away from Uncle Joseph's home in Bristol, and shipped as a common sailor on board the *Shooting Star*, bound for Melbourne. Mrs. Charlton and even the more hopeful Winnie had almost given up expectation of ever hearing of him again. He had reached Melbourne; this they knew, for Uncle Joseph had written to them on the return of the *Shooting Star* to Bristol, but what had become of him after that no one knew. He was without money or friends able to assist him. Doubtless he had perished, like many others, in the bush or at the diggings.

The thought cost poor Mrs. Charlton many a tear, and had caused Winnie to grow graver and older-looking than a girl of seventeen years ought to be. Laura's distressing illness had also been another cause of grief and anxiety, so that both mother and daughter had suffered much since the day Dandie left them to travel to Poland. But the sadness at the Priory had not been an unmixed evil; it had strengthened Mrs. Charlton's naturally weak character; it had developed in Winnie a tender thoughtfulness, which, indeed, had always been hers, but which had increased, until she was truly her mother's right hand and the cherished friend of poor Laura, who, in her childish days, had despised her more staid elder sister.

But Laura was now greatly changed; the pride, the peevishness, the ambition, all seemed to have passed away. She had learned those salutary lessons which sorrow is intended to teach, and she could look up to God, feeling that He was a loving Father still, Who would not send upon her more than she was able to bear. There was, indeed, now much hope that the poor girl would recover the use of her limbs, which she had partially lost since her unfortunate accident on the ice the winter after Dandie had left home. She had received the utmost care and attention, and the best medical advice which money could procure, and the kind author of all this comfort was none other than Uncle Joseph Deane, who, having at last made up his mind to travel down to Scotland to visit his only sister, had been greatly touched by his young niece's suffering condition and by the many signs of poverty which he could not help seeing. Uncle Joseph was not a hard man, though many believed him to be so, but he was terribly afraid of being imposed on. His temper had been soured by the conduct of his own son, and he felt angry at the manner in which Dick had behaved while he was at Bristol. But all anger vanished from his heart when he saw the pale and pretty little Laura lying on a faded couch in the parlour at the Priory, carefully working at some lace, which, when finished, was to be sent to Edinburgh for sale.

'I have earned twenty-five shillings already,' she said, while a flush of pleasure rose on her pale cheek, 'and I do so love to help poor mother.'

Uncle Joseph's heart smote him terribly at these simple words. He was a rich man; twenty-five pounds would have been nothing to him, yet here was his own niece, fragile and delicate, patiently working for long weary hours, in order to lessen her widowed mother's cares. Uncle Joseph felt thoroughly ashamed of himself that he had not sooner made the acquaintance of his sister and her family and shown some attention to these forlorn young girls, who certainly had some claim upon his kindness. But it was not yet too late.

'Sister,' he said, turning hastily round to Mrs. Charlton, 'you must allow me to make this child my peculiar care. She must get the best surgical advice without delay; here, give me pen and paper.' And Uncle Joseph at once wrote a note to the celebrated Professor Syme of Edinburgh, asking him to visit a young patient at St. Andrews. And this was only the beginning of his kind deeds, for when the great surgeon pronounced a favourable verdict, and said that change of air and scene would greatly benefit the young lady, Uncle Joseph would have carried her off then and there to his English home if Winnie could have accompanied her; but this could not be arranged, as Mrs. Charlton had taken two or three young boarders into her family, and she and Winnie were both required to look after them.

'Would you have liked to go with me, my dear?' said Uncle Joseph, looking kindly down upon the girl, whose fair young face was sadly flushed with the excitement of all these arrangements.

'Yes, uncle,' she replied, in rather a hesitating voice; 'but perhaps not for a day or two yet.'

'All right,' said the old man cheerfully; 'then I will go home first, engage an old lady of my acquaintance to take care of you, and you will come this day fortnight. And, sister,' he continued, turning to Mrs. Charlton, 'perhaps you do not know that I have given up my shop now. I mean to rest in my old age, and have taken a house on the Downs at Clifton, where the air is pure and clear, much better than at Bristol. My young niece will thrive there beautifully, I feel perfectly sure.'

Uncle Joseph, having made all these arrangements, took his departure from St. Andrews with a beaming face and a happier heart than he had carried in his bosom since that sad day long, long ago, when his dear young wife had died, leaving him with a baby boy, his son Wilfred. Ah! where was Wilfred now? Was he dead or alive? Had he been too harsh with his boy?

Uncle Joseph's kind plans were duly carried out; Laura was conveyed to his house at Clifton, and placed under the care of Mrs. Austin, a gentle, kindly old lady, whom to know was to love, and who soon made the young invalid feel quite at home.

There is a wonderful difference of temperature

between St. Andrews and Clifton, as Laura speedily discovered after she was removed to Mr. Deane's house; she bloomed out under the more genial skies like a wild rose, until after a few weeks she was able to walk a little, leaning on her uncle's arm. Laura felt very happy: she had known sickness and suffering, and now returning health was very sweet. And if she were happy, what shall we say of Uncle Joseph, whose sole delight it seemed to be to procure pleasures and dainties for his young niece? Indeed, it was well for Laura that her long illness had so much softened and improved her character, for she might otherwise have been thoroughly spoiled at this time by over-kindness. As it was, she took it all very quietly, but often looked so radiant that Uncle Joseph felt greatly pleased.

'Ah, my dear!' he said, 'Clifton agrees with you, that is very easily to be seen. I hope, Laura, you will never speak of going away and leaving your old uncle who loves you.'

And Laura laughingly promised that she would not.

Many a true word is spoken in jest, and the happy young girl did not know that what she promised she really would fulfil; it was her hand that, years after this, was to smooth Uncle Joseph's dying pillow and close his eyes in death.

Such was the state of the Charlton family, when, as already recorded, a letter arrived from poor Dick, the very first letter he had written since he had left Bristol so long before. Mrs. Charlton almost fainted when she saw the well-known handwriting of her boy. With trembling fingers she gave it to Winnie.

'Read it, my dear,' she said; 'tell me, is he well? Where is he? Where is my poor boy?'

But Winnie did not answer; her eyes were running eagerly over the precious paper, till having nearly reached the end of it, she uttered a cry of joy.

'Oh, mother, mother!' she cried, 'such news! you will scarcely be able to believe it! but how our poor Dick must have suffered!'

'Read it, my dear,' answered her mother, 'read it from the very beginning.' And Winnie, almost breathless from excitement, began to read aloud her brother's letter.

It was a very long one, and as our readers are already acquainted with Dick's career up to the time when, sick, miserable, poor, and deserted by his companions, he had risen from his bed in the dim grey of the morning, and turned his back upon the Kajunga diggings for ever, we need only take up his history from that time, and tell it in his own words. The letter was written in a truly penitent style, and contained an account of all his misdeeds, save the one sad and miserable story of Frank Devon's death. Dick did not allude to this, he knew that to hear of anything so dreadful would be anguish to his poor mother's heart, but he did not spare himself in any other particular. After telling how he had left the Kajunga with the earnest desire of beginning a new and better life, he proceeded with his story.

'It was a terrible moment for me when I first left the Creek, for I was still suffering from illness and was entirely without means, all that I possessed being my digger's outfit and tools, and these I was firmly resolved never to use again. I wandered on, taking the first road that presented itself, in the hope of reaching some station where I might procure work for some time, or at least a night's shelter and bread. I fortunately met with a man who purchased my tools from me, giving me as their equivalent some food, flour, coffee, and sugar. This was well for me, as for two nights I had to camp out alone in the bush, and would have been quite destitute of food had it not been for this opportune supply. On the third day of my wanderings, however, I felt very weak and ill, the weather was warm, and the sun seemed literally to burn through my head, while I had not been able for hours to procure a drop of water. Quite suddenly I felt faint and cold, my senses seemed to forsake me, and I fell to the ground, remembering nothing more till I was roused by a friendly voice, and felt the welcome trickling of cold water into my parched throat. I looked up, and met the gaze of a pair of frank and kindly eyes. A young bushman, whose station was close at hand, had been driving home in his dog-cart from visiting his nearest neighbour many miles away, and finding me on the ground, he had promptly come to the rescue. "You will do now, my friend," he said kindly. "You have had just a touch too much of the sun; and now where are you going? Seeking work, I suppose?"

'I told him he had guessed correctly.

'"Well, the day is not so very far off when I was seeking work myself, not five years ago, and now I am in a position to give it to others, so cheer up and come home with me; you need nursing up for a day or two before you will be fit for anything." Mother dear' (so the letter ran), 'you can never know how sweet these words were to me;

I had resolved to try to lead a new and better life, and it really seemed to me at that moment as though God were helping me. My kind deliverer had a small but well-furnished station, and being short of hands he willingly engaged me. I became very fond of him, and the feeling as I afterwards found out was mutual; he had seen that I had been gently born and reared, and very soon he made quite a companion of me. When he had brought me to his house that first day he asked me my name. Mother, I hesitated to tell him, for I felt that I had covered my father's name with disgrace. At last I muttered that my name for the present was Jack Weston.

'"Oh, yes, I see," he replied, cheerfully. "You have not given me your true name for reasons of your own. Well, my name for the present is Charles Chester; every one here knows me by that name, yet it is not my own name, so you see we are in the same box, Jack Weston."

'I pondered over these words, mother, wondering why such a pleasant, frank young fellow should have required to drop his family name; he could not have behaved so badly as I had done, I felt sure of that. At last I ceased to think of it, I stuck to my work, had good wages, and as I had quite given up drink I soon began to save money. This pleased Mr. Chester, and he became more friendly than ever. "Jack," he said to me one day, "you are very useful to me. I will make you my partner in the concern at least to this extent, that when I am away from home, you will be 'Boss' and get a share of the profits. Now I must go to Melbourne shortly, and I expect to be there for some time. Can you take charge in my absence, do you think?"

'"If the men will be ruled by me," I replied; "but it is not so long since I was upon the same level as themselves."

'"I will make that all right with the men," Mr. Chester said. "And I dare say you will get on very well."

'Mother, just think how gratified I felt at all this; had Mr. Chester been my own brother I could scarcely have loved him more. Well, it was all arranged, and the day fixed for his departure to Melbourne, when an unexpected and sorrowful event took place. One evening Mr. Chester was taken ill; he had been overheated while riding, and then had caught a chill. Inflammation set in, and he was soon in a precarious condition. I had sent for the nearest doctor, twelve miles off, but my messenger returned saying the doctor had gone to Melbourne. I nursed Mr. Chester as well as I could; we had not a woman about the place, so I was single-handed. One night I feared it was all up with him, and he seemed to think so himself, for he beckoned me to his bedside, and looked fixedly in my face.

'"Jack," he said, "I fear I may not get over this. I cannot die without telling you who I am, and asking you to write to my friends in the old country. Oh, Jack, I have been a bad son!"

'For a minute or two he could say no more, so I tried to cheer him up a bit; but he stopped me.

'"Let me get on with my confession, lest I get too weak to speak. Jack, you will write to my father, and tell him that I have long since repented of my folly and ingratitude, that I truly grieve to think how I must have pained his heart, for I know he loved me. Oh, Jack, when we are very ill these thoughts are agony!"

'Mother, I could not say it to him then, but well did I know the agony of remorse for a wicked past. As I did not speak, he went on, "You promise me, Jack? That is good. I have written my father's address down on this paper," and he handed it to me with his trembling fingers. But judge of my astonishment when I read, " Mr. Joseph Deane, Spice Merchant, Savory Street, Bristol." '

Here Winnie had to stop reading; agitation and excitement choked her utterance, while her mother was in tears.

'Oh, my poor dear brother, what news this will be to him! Winnie, can you imagine it? The two cousins meeting, and having lived together so long without knowing each other. Does it not seem strange?'

'No, mother, I think not,' said Winnie. 'Remember that both Dick and Mr. Chester, or Cousin Wilfred as I must now call him, were bent on concealing their antecedents. They would not talk of the old home life at all, and then they had never met.'

'True,' replied Mrs. Charlton; 'but it just reads like a novel. Go on, Winnie, my dear, let me hear the end of it.'

'Yes, mother,' said Winnie, with a smile; 'you have something more to hear. Oh, mother, this is a joyful day!' and she resumed her reading of Dick's long and interesting letter.

'When I read Uncle Joseph's well-known address, and knew that Mr. Chester was no other than my Cousin Wilfred, his son, who had run away from home years before, I can scarcely tell you, mother, how I felt, the old days came so vividly back upon me. I must have shown some agitation, for he looked up in my face, and asked me anxiously what was the matter. Mother, I thought it best to conceal nothing. I told him who I was. I told him how Uncle Joseph, after making me a most generous offer, and taking me into his house, had again been disappointed in me. I told him how insolently I had treated my uncle, and finally, how I, too, had run away, and sailed in the *Shooting Star* for Melbourne. Poor Wilfred almost shed tears over my story.

'"Oh, my poor father!" he said; "disappointed for the second time, and left alone in his old age! Oh, Cousin Dick, may God give us both grace to repent! He was a kind, generous father to me, though perhaps a little stern. I have heard that my poor mother's death almost broke his heart; some men never get over these sorrows. But, please God, if I get over this illness, I will go home and beg my poor father to forgive the past and be reconciled. I know that he loved me."

'Here Wilfred, quite exhausted, lay back and closed his eyes. I almost thought he was gone; but God was very good to us. He soon rallied, and from that day began to amend. And now, dear mother, here comes the most interesting part of my story, and the part which most nearly concerns myself. As soon as Wilfred was restored to health, he told me that he was in a strangely restless state of mind, that night and day he seemed to see his old father's face looking beseechingly at him, and that he had quite resolved to go home.

'"Dick," he said, "if my father were to die now, before I was reconciled to him and had got his forgiveness, I really think it would break my heart!"

'I suggested that he should write to his father, but he said no, a letter was never so satisfactory as an interview, and he was quite resolved upon going home. "And now, Dick," he said, "what about yourself? I mean to sell the station; indeed, I already know a man who is willing to take it off my hands, and give a good price for it, too. Now, what will you do?"

'Of course, mother, I felt quite at a standstill; Wilfred going away altered things terribly for me. I had saved up a few hundred pounds, but what to do next I really could not make up my mind.

'"Cousin," said Wilfred, kindly, "you have

money enough to pay your passage home and more; go home with me. My father will get you employment of some kind, I know he will. And even if he did not, I will see that you do not want. Why, Dick, by your kind nursing you have, I believe, saved my life," and the good fellow wrung my hand. Mother, do you see it now? I am coming home, we are both coming home, and will be with you almost as soon as you get this letter! Dear mother, you will receive your repentant son? I know you will. And you must write and tell Uncle Joseph all these astounding news. Dear Winnie! how I long to see her, and naughty little Laura! And what is Dandie doing? Has he got any employment? But of course he has; he would never remain idle all this time. Whatever he is about, I feel sure that he is a better son to you than I have ever been. But the future is before me, and with God's help I hope to redeem the past.

'Your ever-loving and repentant son,
'RICHARD CHARLTON.'

At the close of this long and interesting letter Mrs. Charlton and Winnie wept together, but the tears were those of joy. How changed everything seemed now that the prodigal had come to his right mind!

'My dear,' said Mrs. Charlton, 'he says that he may be with us almost as soon as we get his letter. What if they should arrive this very day! Oh, Winnie, run and open the spare room window, and give out sheets, my dear, to be well aired; and, oh, Winnie, could you not make a veal pie, just to be ready, my dear?'

'But Uncle Joseph should be written to first, mother; just think what these news will be to him,' said Winnie, thoughtfully.

'Of course, my dear, you are right. What would I do without you? Give me my desk. I will write to him myself. Meanwhile, dear, don't forget about the sheets and the pie.'

But these words were scarcely uttered when the little servant-maid entered the room, carrying a telegram between her finger and thumb, as though afraid it might bite her. Winnie seized it in a moment.

'Mother,' she cried, 'the ship is in London, and they are going to Bristol first, as it is so much nearer than here. They hope you have told Uncle Joseph. They will be in London two days.'

Here was a dilemma! Uncle Joseph knew

nothing as yet, but Mrs. Charlton's pen was soon rushing over the paper, while Winnie, feeling that the pie might now rest for a little, retired to her own room in a tumult of joy that she might write all the wonderful news to her dear brother Dandie. Unsuspecting Winnie!

'Laura, my dear, here is a very thick and weighty letter from your mother. Read it, my darling, and then you must get ready for your drive with me; the air is quite delightful to-day, for the season. When you are ready, you will find me in the garden,' and so saying Uncle Joseph went off to look at his crocuses, which were just appearing above ground.

Presently Laura appeared, but not dressed for a drive; she wore a warm shawl, covering head and shoulders, and looked rather pale.

'Uncle,' she said, 'this is mother's letter; you must read it, uncle, please.'

'Read your mother's letter! No, indeed, my dear, her letters are sacred to yourself; never suppose, Laura, that I want to read your letters.'

'Oh, but, uncle, please read this one, it concerns yourself, mother sent it for you to read,' and she put it into his hands and then disappeared. She wanted Uncle Joseph to be alone when he heard of his long-lost son. Ah, what thoughts were stirred in his heart when he read Dick's long and truly wonderful letter! The truants had met in the wilds of Australia, and were coming home together! What a welcome they would receive! What joy, what gratitude filled the old man's heart! How he resolved that not only his son, but his widowed sister and her children would thenceforth be dear to his heart! If they would just love him a little, it was all he would ask; he would do everything to make them happy and comfortable; his wealth he would use for their benefit—they should all be to him as his own children. He might yet have a future of happiness in his old age, after the loveless past!

He left the garden and returned to the house, that he might go over the wonderful story with Mrs. Austin and his niece. He knew how pleased Laura must be to hear of her brother Dick's return.

Scarcely had he reached the garden gate, when he was confronted by a tall sun-browned man, whose eyes seemed strangely familiar to him, and who looked yearningly in his face, while a younger man stood behind. It was the two truants, the runaway lads, and in another moment Wilfred Deane was in his father's arms.

CHAPTER XI

A DISTINGUISHED GUEST

WE must now return to Hamburg where we left Dandie with an unwonted gravity on his young face, sitting by Count Emile's bed, and very anxiously pondering this very difficult query, 'What was next to be done?' And truly his position at this time was a somewhat unpleasant one. Up to this moment he had been the victim of circumstances—he had had no choice—no time even to choose. When the sudden discovery of Louis' treachery had made the immediate flight of the young Count necessary he had promised to the Countess that he would ride to the frontier with her son, but nothing further had been arranged, no time being left for other plans, with the wild Cossacks already on their trail. He had left the Château without a word of farewell to Count Demetrius; he had left all his own worldly possessions behind him. What else could he have done?

Having reached the frontier, they could not, of course, stay there, challenged by Russia on the one hand, and Prussia on the other; therefore, after bribing the Prussian guards, they had thankfully fled to Hamburg, where, as it was a free city, they could not be molested. But now, what next? Dandie's own resources were but small, Emile's bag of gold was sadly diminished. Poland was now, of course, closed to both of them; they did not even dare to write to the Countess, lest they might bring her and Count Demetrius into trouble, and most certainly they could not remain long at Hamburg without money.

In these circumstances Dandie felt that he was limited to one course, he must take his unfortunate friend to his mother's house at St. Andrews. The Priory Cottage was not very large certainly, but a warm welcome would make up for all deficiencies, and of a warm welcome Dandie felt quite sure. Still, it would not do to burden his mother too long; he must think of some secure refuge for Count Emile, and of some new employment for himself. These were all very weighty and pressing questions, and Dandie felt almost overpowered with the burden of them.

At last his mind was made up; he remembered

the friendly old man who had taken him to the wolf-hunt, Count Stanislas Praga, the intimate friend of the Slavonski family; he knew that he had taken no part in the late revolt of the Poles, and, therefore, would probably be unmolested by the Russian Government. To him he would write, entreating him to see the Countess, and assure her of her son's safety, also requesting his advice as to the young Count's future movements, concluding his letter by giving Count Praga his mother's address at St. Andrews. This letter being written Dandie felt much more at ease, and he now turned his attention with a cheerful face to his Polish friend. But here was a new dilemma! Count Emile had been reflecting, too, and had in consequence fallen into a condition of the saddest despondency, so much so that he seemed scarcely able to take an interest in any one thing. The first fever-heat of excitement had passed away with the wild ride across the frontier; time for reflection had come, and Emile's reflections were sad in the extreme.

'Ah, my friend!' he said, as he caught Dandie's hand, 'it is impossible for you to know what I feel; you are one of a brave, free people, to whom tyranny and oppression are unknown; you have only to form your own plans, and then carry them out without let or hindrance, but I . . . Ah, poor Poland! brave, yet oppressed, ever struggling, yet never free! My friend, I should not have come with you; I have brought trouble upon you, I can see it in your face. I have brought ruin upon my father and mother, for I know their property will now be confiscated in revenge for my escape; better, far better had I been content to suffer and to die in the Caucasus among my country's enemies.'

But Dandie would not listen to any more of this kind of talk, though deeply sympathizing with his friend's very natural feelings of distress. He therefore set himself to the task of cheering up the young Count.

'You must not despond,' he said; 'you must be hopeful and look forward to better days. I give you the advice which my sister gave to me when I was looking sadly forward to a future which seemed to promise me nothing. "Trust in God, and do the right." It was right to try to save your life, and it was right that I should do what I could to help you. Now let us both trust in God, and He will not fail us, we may feel sure of that.'

As Emile seemed to be somewhat cheered by the

hopefulness of his English friend he complained no more, but expressed himself as ready to make any move suggested by Dandie, who then sat down to write his second letter to the beloved mother and sister, who, as yet, believed him to be quietly settled with Count Demetrius in Poland.

It would be difficult to describe the feelings of Mrs. Charlton and Winnie when this letter arrived at the Priory Cottage, so soon after that exciting and delightful letter from Dick which had filled their hearts with so much joy. What astonishment was theirs when they read of the grand ride across the frontier! what a hero was Dandie in their eyes! how proud they felt of his bravery and unselfishness! how glad they would be to embrace their hero once more! Still, there was a reverse side to this picture. Poor Dandie had sacrificed all his prospects; where could he find employment now? Then the knowledge that they were expected to entertain a Polish fugitive and a man of rank gave them no little perplexity.

Mrs. Charlton's thoughts (like most mothers) immediately ran off to the consideration of ways and means. The cottage was small; where ought she to lodge her distinguished guest? Would the tiny garret-room be suitable for Dandie? and, oh, what a difficulty she would feel if Dick should come just at once to visit her, and perhaps bring Wilfred Deane along with him! How could she ever hope to accommodate at one time so many guests? But in the midst of these perplexing thoughts, the poor lady felt that she had, indeed, much to be grateful for; her two dear boys were both alive and well, though both had gone through many strange adventures since they had left the shelter of her roof. She had Winnie, too—dear, considerate, kind Winnie—with her useful hands and her thoughtful head. Ah, what an unspeakable solace to a widowed mother is a good, kind, unselfish daughter!

'And now, Winnie, that I have got you to myself for five precious minutes, tell me what you think of Count Emile; and please speak respectfully of him —remember that he is your brother's friend.' So spoke Dandie Charlton, as he walked with his favourite sister along Eagle's Cliff, about a fortnight after his return home, recalling with interest and almost amusement the thoughts and emotions of the far-off past—for when we are young 'two years ago,' especially if they have been eventful years, seem a far-off past indeed.

Winnie laughed. 'I think him a very pleasant

young man,' she replied. 'I do not feel so overwhelmed by the Countship as I expected to be; he is extravagantly polite, especially to mother, who is quite delighted with him; he talks wonderfully good English, which is just as well, for my French is wofully deficient; he is handsome, no one can deny that, good-looking, well-mannered; his voice is sweet, he sings well; the slight tinge of melancholy, which one cannot but perceive, only enhances——'

'Hold hard, Winnie!' cried Dandie, who began to feel jealous of his friend. 'I am quite satisfied with your appreciation of Emile; don't carry it too far, my dear.'

Winnie laughed again. 'You seemed so very anxious to have him regarded in a favourable light, Dandie, that I tried to sum up all his good points for your benefit; but to speak truthfully he seems to be an amiable, though rather sad-hearted, young man. We cannot wonder at his feelings, of course; his poor mother! she must be thinking of him night and day. What do you think he ought to do, Dandie?'

'That is just what I want to talk about,' said her brother. 'I brought you here because I want to consult you, Winnie. A wonderful amount of wisdom lies in that golden head of yours. Now, Winnie, listen; I have received a letter from Count Praga, and he makes proposals which may alter all my future life. I may be going away from home once more.'

'Away from home!' echoed Winnie, rather sadly. 'Back to Poland, Dandie?'

'Certainly not,' replied her brother, decidedly. 'Poland has seen the last of me, unless I choose to run the risk of a Russian prison. But I will read the letter to you, Winnie, for I rely greatly on your advice and sympathy, my dear.'

The letter was a long one, and as interesting as it was long. Count Praga, who was an enthusiastic old man, began by praising his young English friend—his bravery, his unselfishness, his heroism—to all of which Winnie listened with fullest sympathy. Then the Count proceeded to tell how he had seen Emile's mother, and relieved her anxiety about her son. He had found the Château almost dismantled, all the servants gone, save two faithful adherents of the family. The Russian police had been there; they had searched the whole mansion, and had carried away private papers, and, indeed, everything that took their fancy. In short, all the Count's property had been confiscated; he was a ruined man, the police assuring him that he might consider himself fortunate in that he had not been sent to Siberia.

Here Winnie interrupted the reading of Count Praga's letter. 'Oh, Dandie, how dreadful! Have you told Count Emile this sad news of his parents? How it will distress him!'

'Oh, bother Count Emile!' said Dandie, rather irritably. 'You are a soft-hearted little goose, Winnie; don't interrupt me again.' And he went on with the letter, while a tiny pink flush rose in Winnie's fair cheek. Dandie had never been so cross before. Surely Poland had not improved him!

But the letter grew so very interesting that Winnie forgot her momentary annoyance in listening to it. Count Praga went on to say that he himself felt sadly distressed by the state of matters in the Slavonski household; he was broken-hearted too at the hopeless condition of Poland, and felt that he could no longer be happy in the land of his birth; he intended to emigrate to America, where so many of his countrymen had already settled, and he had persuaded Count Demetrius to go with him. 'I am a rich man,' he continued, 'and have no family to provide for.

I therefore gladly offer an asylum to those dear friends of my youth who have been more cruelly treated by the Russian Government than I have been. My home will be pitched far away from cities, in the wild free West, where one can breathe freely, and can watch the sun setting over miles and miles of forest trees. To live in a city would stifle me, and Count Demetrius feels as I do in this respect. And now about my young friend Emile. His dear mother pines to see him, but to Poland he cannot return, while we ourselves will have turned our backs upon it for ever in a few weeks. Emile must follow us to America; he will be heartily welcomed by me; and that he should do so is the earnest wish of his parents also, which Emile is too good a son to refuse. And now in concluding, my dear young friend, I speak for Count Demetrius as well as myself when I say that if we can advance your interests in any way we will gladly do so. We owe you a debt of gratitude which nothing can ever repay. If you will accompany Emile to America, nothing could be better. We shall see that you get remunerative employment, and your home will be with us. Think over it, and let me know your decision by an early post.'

A silence of a few minutes followed the reading

of Count Praga's letter, and then Winnie spoke. 'And are you really going, Dandie?'

'I think so, my dear,' replied her brother. 'I have no other prospect before me; and now that Dick is in England, and likely to do well, there is no reason why I should remain in this country. Of course, I shall be sorry to leave my mother and you; still, having already been away from home for two years, I think I have grown restless, Winnie. I could not remain at St. Andrews. I want more elbow-room, my dear. Oh, Winnie, child, don't cry! I hate to see girls crying, and why should you do so? You could not wish me to remain at home idle, Winnie!'

No, Winnie did not expect nor wish anything so foolish, still the tears would come. Winnie felt that they were all upon the eve of great changes; the dear old home-life, when they were boys and girls, was already a thing of the past. Laura was already away; Dick was to remain at Bristol in partnership with Wilfred Deane; and now Dandie was going, and, worse still, he was glad to go, he was restless and weary of home! No one left at the Priory but herself and dear mother; oh, it did seem sad! But she soon came to a better state of mind.

'I should not grieve, dear **Dandie**,' she said. 'I fear I am just a little selfish; but we shall miss you so much, you and the Count; you have enlivened our evenings, and made us all so happy, so very happy!' Poor dear little Winnie.

CHAPTER XII

BRIGHTER DAYS

But Dandie was not going away quite immediately; it takes time to arrange matters so important as these, and Winnie had time for many another walk with her brother on the Eagle's Cliff, or in the environs of St. Andrews, before the time came for the parting. On one of these occasions, as brother and sister were walking together and engaged in earnest conversation about Dandie's prospects in America, they were met by a young girl, who, after a shy glance at Dandie, bowed to Winnie and passed on her way.

'What girl is that to whom you bowed, Winnie?' said her brother; 'it seems to me that I have seen her before.'

'Of course you have seen her before,' cried Winnie. 'Why, she is Effie Moncrieff; don't you remember her? She was Laura's little school friend when they attended the Madras Academy together at the time of our father's death.'

'Is that Effie Moncrieff?' exclaimed Dandie, in astonishment. 'How changed she is! how much she has grown! Is she Laura's friend still?'

'Oh, indeed, yes!' said Winnie. 'When poor Laura first met with her accident I do not know how she would have been able to bear it had it not been for Effie: she came so often to see her, and was so sympathizing and unselfish. Although she is a year younger than Laura she exercised a good influence over her, and I am sure greatly helped to improve Laura's character. You should go and call on the Moncrieffs, Dandie, they live in the same house still in North Street; Mrs. Moncrieff has been much of an invalid for some months past, but I am sure she would be glad to see you.'

'But I have so much to arrange and think about, I have no time for paying visits,' replied her brother. 'I wish I had time to go to Bristol to see Uncle Joseph and Dick, but I have neither time nor money to spend in running up and down the country. I almost wonder, Winifred, that Dick has never come here yet to see mother; I am sure she must feel hurt at his neglect.'

'Oh dear, no!' cried Winnie, eagerly; 'did you

not know that she had a letter from Dick this morning? It is Uncle Joseph who will not allow him to come as yet; there are some business matters to be settled; you know uncle is very particular about business being attended to; but Dick is to be here next week. Poor fellow! he must have suffered most terribly when he was in Australia, and he is so ready to blame himself now, so different to what he used to be! But, see! there comes mother to meet us, and Count Emile. It is quite amusing, Dandie, to see how fond he is of mother!'

'And of some one else, too, or I am much mistaken!' thought Dandie, as he critically watched Emile's animated face on meeting Winnie. 'What an ass he is after all! Does he really think that though mother is blind I do not see through him? It is quite absurd that he should be running after Winnie like this!'

Dick's first visit home would have been almost painful to him, so acutely did he remember all the foolish and sinful past, had it not been arranged that Uncle Joseph, Wilfred, and Laura should all go with him to spend a few days at St. Andrews; this influx of visitors causing such an excitement at the Priory that Dick escaped from the pain of being the object of too much attention. Still, when he first met Dandie and was introduced to Count Emile, Dick did feel very small indeed. What a contrast there was between him and his brother! how noble had been Dandie's conduct! how unworthy his own! If at any moment he caught the eye of Count Emile he always felt that the same thought must be running in the mind of the young Pole; but this was a mistake on his part. Emile had heard nothing whatever of Dick's Australian adventures, he looked upon him merely as another member of the most delightful family he had ever met. For Emile at this time was very happy with the Charlton family; his mind was so far at rest about his parents and his own future, he had therefore thrown off all his perplexing cares for the moment, and had given himself up to the harmless pleasures of the present.

Uncle Joseph had taken lodgings for himself, Wilfred, and Laura as near the Priory as possible; and as it was the pleasantest season of the year—early summer—many delightful walking and boating excursions were enjoyed by the large party of young people, who, as is the custom of youth, resolutely shut their eyes to the painful fact that very soon now the inevitable separation must come.

Uncle Joseph and his family would shortly return to Clifton, while Dandie and Count Emile would proceed to their new and untried home in the Far West, where Count Praga and Emile's parents were already established.

Our story draws to a close; but before we say farewell to our friends, whose varying fortunes we have followed so far, we must take one parting glance at them all in their different homes, bearing in mind that the long period of five years has elapsed since we saw the large and happy party of young people assembled together at St. Andrews.

And first let us look in at the Priory, where we have so often been before. Alas! it is deserted now by one and all. Another family occupies its chambers, and other children play in its old-fashioned garden, or scamper along the Eagle's Cliff. The place that once knew the Charlton family knows them no more. We shall therefore ask our readers to accompany us to Clifton, and see how many of them are to be found in Uncle Joseph's comfortable and roomy dwelling-house on the breezy Downs.

First of all what of Uncle Joseph himself? for our young readers, we feel sure, are not indifferent to the fate of the old man, who, although he was somewhat harsh and stern at one time, yet afterwards grew so kind and gentle that the young people, one and all, loved him sincerely. Well, it was the middle of summer, blue skies, white fleecy clouds sailing here and there, with flowers of every hue scenting the air with perfume. Uncle Joseph was a great lover of his garden, cultivating roses especially, till he had them everywhere, climbing up the front of his house, mingled with jessamine and ivy, or growing as standards in trim, well-cared-for beds. But he pays little attention to them now, and, indeed, has handed them over to Wilfred's care, for poor Uncle Joseph is closely confined to the house, and seldom leaves his own bedroom. It would have been sad for him now had he been all alone, as he had been when both Wilfred and Dick had run away from him. But he is no longer alone. Wilfred is as his right hand, attending to all business matters, while Laura looks after the comfort of the dear invalid's daily life, and sees that his every wish is immediately gratified. And Laura is not only his niece and dear little housekeeper, she is the happy wife of his son, Wilfred, who remembers with gratitude the day when he found Dick Charlton lying nearly dead in the Australian bush; it was through this apparently chance encounter that he was restored to his place in his father's home and heart, and which led to his knowing the cousin whom he quickly learned to love.

Uncle Joseph is very near his end now, and he knows it; and though life is dear to all of us, he is not unwilling to quit all and go, for he has learned to look up with faith, and to see a Father and a Home in Heaven. Uncle Joseph is happy, as we all shall be if, when we come to die, we possess his faith and trust in our Heavenly Father's love!

But where is Dick? surely he has not again become unsteady and left his kind uncle's roof! No, Dick is prospering, as all those who try to do well deserve to prosper. He and Wilfred are partners in a great paper-making concern, and are quickly becoming rich men. But the paper-mill is at least fifteen miles away from Clifton, and it has been arranged that Dick should reside there with weekly visits to Clifton, while Wilfred remains at Clifton with weekly visits to the mill. Both young men are fast friends. And is Laura happy? Oh, so happy! as every one must be who has some one else to love and care for; and she knows herself to be very necessary to the comfort of the household. Besides, has she not another sweet source of joy and happiness in the dear little curly-haired boy who looks up in her face and calls her mother? The old merchant's house on the Clifton Downs is truly a happy one!

And now we must cross the wide and stormy Atlantic and look in upon our old friends Count Demetrius Slavonski, and the lady his wife, the genial old Count Praga, Dandie, and his friend, Count Emile. We cannot expect to find all these under one roof, neither would it have been desirable; the old and the young have different tastes, and are sometimes apt to interfere with each other's comfort. But we will look in upon them all and see what they are all about. Count Demetrius Slavonski has aged much during these five years of residence in America; of all our refugees he is the one who has suffered most by an enforced emigration from his own country. But he is happy in a way, chiefly in having his beloved wife with him still, and in knowing that his son Emile can never again fall into the hands of his Russian foes. But his thoughts continually revert to beloved Poland, and no place can ever be to him so dear. What does it matter that it has no particular beauty to attract attention? that its surface is one wide level plain with many a tract of marsh or barren heath, intersected by miles on miles of dreary forest, buried for five months of the year in a wilderness of snow? Home is home wherever it may be! and it is a sad thing for any one of us when the love of country dies out of our hearts.

Count Praga is a man of another stamp; bright and genial, he sees the good side of everything. Poland is still dear, but seeing that he could not remain there any longer with comfort, why, America is not so very bad; there are level tracts of land enough and to spare; there are forests enough to satisfy even a Polish nobleman, and certainly there is snow enough and to spare. Yes, Count Praga enjoys life wonderfully, and is never so happy as when with his own rod or gun he can supply the family table with fish and wild game.

Count Emile, if questioned, would declare himself to be the happiest of them all. His home is a lovely ornamental cottage, not very far from the larger dwelling-house of Count Praga, and much more beautifully situated. Surrounded by prettily laid out grounds, at the end of which runs a bright, clear river, whose banks slope gradually up into a hill densely covered with pines, which, in the fierce heat of an American summer, look deliciously cool and shady, while their health-giving scent perfumes the air all around. It is a sweet and lovely spot, and rendered all the dearer to Emile as it is presided over by his fair young English wife, our old acquaintance, Winifred Charlton. For some time Dandie felt some dislike to the idea of his friend's marriage to his favourite sister, but as brothers are sometimes a little eccentric in such matters Winnie generously forgave him.

Dandie himself is the moving spirit of the little Anglo-Polish colony. He superintends everything, is brisk, sensible, energetic, and kind-hearted as ever; but, alas! he has no helpmeet, and begins to think that a single life, however busy, is a mistake. It has been reported, however, that he intends to pay a holiday visit to St. Andrews, Scotland, and it will not be Winnie's fault if he does not bring back with him as his bride Laura's little school friend of the olden days, Effie Moncrieff. And now we have given a true and particular account of every one of our friends, save one, Mrs. Charlton herself.

It is never pleasant to end a story with anything sad, but in this case we must do so, though why should it be sad to record the death of one who died happily? In a small cemetery on the hill-side above Count Emile's house, a sweet and secluded spot, Mrs. Charlton lies at rest; her last words to her children and friends being these: 'God has been very good; trust Him, my dear ones, trust Him only, and trust Him always.' And thus we close the history of the Charlton Family.

THE END

WELLS GARDNER, DARTON AND CO., PATERNOSTER BUILDINGS.

www.ingramcontent.com/pod-product-compliance
Lightning Source LLC
Chambersburg PA
CBHW030318170426
43202CB00009B/1050